Rite Aid
# GUIDE TO HEALTH

# Stress Management

*Practical Ways to Relax
and Be Healthy*

EVE ADAMSON

Published by
Adams Media, an F+W Publications Company
57 Littlefield Street
Avon, MA 02322
*www.adamsmedia.com*

ISBN 10: 1-59337-695-2
ISBN 13: 978-1-59337-695-6

Printed in Canada.

J  I  H  G  F  E  D  C  B

**Library of Congress Cataloging-in-Publication Data**
available from the publisher.

This book includes material from *The Everything* Stress Management Book* by
Eve Adamson, ©2002, F+W Publications, Inc.

*Rite Aid Guide to Health: Stress Management* is intended as a reference volume
only, not as a medical manual. In light of the complex, individual, and specific nature of health problems, this book is not intended to replace professional medical advice. The ideas, procedures, and suggestions in this book are
intended to supplement, not replace, the advice of a trained medical professional. Consult your physician before adopting the suggestions in this book.
The author and publisher disclaim any liability arising directly or indirectly
from the use of this book.

This publication is designed to provide accurate and authoritative information with regard to the subject matter covered. It is sold with the understanding that the publisher is not engaged in rendering legal, accounting, or other
professional advice. If legal advice or other expert assistance is required, the
services of a competent professional person should be sought.
   —From a *Declaration of Principles* jointly adopted by a Committee of the
American Bar Association and a Committee of Publishers and Associations

Many of the designations used by manufacturers and sellers to distinguish
their product are claimed as trademarks. Where those designations appear in
this book and Adams Media was aware of a trademark claim, the designations
have been printed with initial capital letters.

# Contents

# Introduction

So, you think you're stressed? At least you're in good company! Stress has become a national epidemic, but knowing everyone else around you is suffering as much as you isn't much help when your muscles are tense, your mind is racing, your palms are sweaty, your stomach hurts, and you can't concentrate on any of many items on your monumental to-do list.

Luckily, there is hope for you and everyone who suffers from stress. You just need a little training in stress management, and you've come to the right place. You can manage your stress, and you don't have to do it alone. With a little guidance, inspiration, and a commitment to help yourself so that you can be your best possible self, you can be feeling better soon. So relax. Take a deep breath. Put your feet up on your desk and crack open this book. Stress doesn't stand a chance.

*Chapter 1*

# Stress Unmasked

You know you're under stress
when you rear-end a car on
the way to work (oops!), make
it to work three hours late and
get fired (no!), then have your
wallet stolen on the bus ride
home (oh, that's just perfect!).
But is it stressful to graduate
from college, start an exercise
program, or binge on cookies?
You bet it is.

## What Is Stress?

What's so stressful about a few chocolate chip cookies? Nothing, if you eat two chocolate chip cookies every day as part of a well-balanced diet. Plenty, if you deprive yourself of desserts for a month, then eat an entire bag of double fudge chocolate chunk. You aren't used to all those cookies. Your body isn't used to all that sugar. That's stressful. Not stressful like totaling your car or getting transferred to Siberia, but stressful nonetheless.

In the same way, anything out of the ordinary that happens to you is stressful on your body.

Some stress feels good. Even great. Without any stress at all, life would be a big bore.

Stress isn't, by definition, something bad, but it certainly isn't always good, either. In fact, it can cause dramatic health problems if it happens to you too much and for too long.

Stress isn't just out-of-the-ordinary stuff, however. Stress can also be hidden and deeply embedded in your life. What if you can't stand your job in middle management but continue to go there every day because you're afraid of starting your own business and giving up the regular paycheck? What if your family has serious communication problems, or if you live in a place where you don't feel safe? Maybe everything seems just fine, but nevertheless you feel deeply unhappy. Even when you are accustomed to certain things in your life—dirty dishes in the sink, family members that don't help you out, twelve-hour days at the office—those things can be stressful. You might even get stressed out when something goes right. Maybe someone is nice to you and you become suspicious, or you feel uncomfortable if your house is too clean. You are so used to things being difficult that you don't know how to adjust. Stress is a strange and highly individual phenomenon.

Unless you live in a cave without a television (actually, not a bad way to eliminate stress in your life), you've probably heard quite a bit about stress in the media, around the coffee machine at work, or in the magazines and newspapers you read. Most people have a preconceived notion of what stress is in general, as well as what stress is to them.

### *What does stress mean to you?*

- Discomfort?
- Pain?
- Worry?
- Anxiety?
- Excitement?
- Fear?
- Uncertainty?

These things cause people stress and are mostly conditions stemming from stress. But what is stress itself? Stress is such a broad term, and there are so many different kinds of stress affecting so many people in so many different ways that the word stress may seem to defy definition. What is stressful to one person might be exhilarating to another. So, what exactly is stress?

Stress comes in several guises, some more obvious than others. Some stress is acute, some is episodic, and some is chronic. Let's take a closer look at each kind of stress and how it affects you.

## When Life Changes: Acute Stress

Acute stress is the most obvious kind of stress, and it's pretty easy to spot if you associate it with one thing: Change.

Yep, that's all it is. Change. Stuff you're not used to. And that can include anything, from a change in your diet to a change in your exercise habits to a change in your job to a change in the people involved in your life, whether you've lost them or gained them.

In other words, acute stress is something that disturbs your body's equilibrium. You get used to things being a certain way, physically, mentally, emotionally, even chemically. Your body clock is set to sleep at certain times, your energy rises and falls at certain times, and your blood sugar changes in response to the meals you eat at certain times each day. As you go along your merry way in life, entrenched in your routines and habits and "normal" way of living, your body and your mind know pretty much what to expect.

But when something happens to change our existence, whether that something is a physical change (like a cold virus or a sprained ankle), a chemical change (like the side effects of a medication or the hormonal fluctuations following childbirth), or an emotional change (like a marriage, a child leaving the nest, or the death of a loved one), our equilibrium is altered. Our life changes. Our bodies and minds are thrown out of the routine they've come to expect. We've experienced change, and with that comes stress.

Acute stress is hard on our bodies and our minds because people tend to be creatures of habit. Even the most spontaneous and schedule resistant among us have our habits, and habits don't just mean enjoying that morning cup of coffee or sleeping on that favorite side of the bed. Habits include minute, complex, intricate interworkings of physical, chemical, and emotional factors on our bodies.

Say you get up and go to work five days each week, rising at 6:00 A.M., downing a bagel and a cup of coffee, then hopping on the subway. Once a year, you go on vacation, and, for two weeks, you sleep until 11:00 A.M., then wake up and eat a staggering brunch. That's stressful, too, because you've changed your habits. You probably enjoy it, and in some ways, a vacation can mediate the chronic stress of sleep deprivation.

But if you are suddenly sleeping different hours and eating different things than usual, your body clock will have to readjust, your blood chemistry will have to readjust, and just when you've readjusted, you'll probably have to go back to waking up at 6:00 A.M. and foregoing the daily bacon and cheese omelets for that good old bagel again. That's not to say you shouldn't go on vacation. You certainly shouldn't avoid all change.

Humans desire and need a certain degree of change. Without change, life wouldn't be much fun.

Change makes life exciting and memorable. Change can be fun . . . up to a point.

Here's the tricky part: How much change you can stand before the changes start to have a negative effect on you is a completely individual issue. A certain amount of stress is good, but too much will start to become unhealthy, unsettling, and unbalancing. No single formula will calculate what "too much stress" is for everyone because the level of acute stress you can stand is likely to be completely different than the level of stress your friends and relatives can stand (although a low level of stress tolerance does appear to be inheritable).

## When Life Is a Roller Coaster: Episodic Stress

Episodic stress is like lots of acute stress—in other words, lots of life changes—all at once and over a period of time. People who suffer from episodic stress always seem to be in the throes of some tragedy. They tend to be overwrought, sometimes intense, often irritable, angry, or anxious.

If you've ever been through a week, a month, even a year when you seemed to suffer personal disaster after personal disaster, you know what it's like to be in the throes of episodic stress. First, your furnace breaks down, then you bounce a check, then you get a speeding ticket, then your entire extended family decides to stay with you for four weeks, then your sister-in-law smashes into your garage with her car, and then you get the flu. For some people, episodic stress becomes so drawn out a process that they become used to it; to others, the stress state is obvious. "Oh, that poor woman. She has terrible luck!" "Did you hear what happened to Jerry this time?"

Episodic stress, like acute stress, can also come in more positive forms. First, a whirlwind courtship, a huge wedding, a honeymoon in Bali, buying a new home, and moving in with your new spouse for the first time, all in the same year, is an incredibly stressful sequence of events. Fun, sure. Romantic, yes. Even thrilling. But still an excellent example of episodic stress in its sunnier, though no less stressful, manifestation.

Sometimes, episodic stress comes in a more subtle form—such as "worry." Worry is like inventing stress, or change, before it happens, even when it has little chance of happening. Excessive worry could be linked to an anxiety disorder, but even when worry is less chronic than that, it saps the body's energy, usually for no good reason.

> Worry is usually just the contemplation of horrible things that are extremely unlikely to happen. Worry doesn't solve problems.

Worry puts your body under stress by creating or imagining changes in the equilibrium of life—changes that haven't even happened!

Are you a worrywart? How many of the following describe you?

- You find yourself worrying about things that are extremely unlikely, such as suffering from a freak accident or developing an illness you have no reason to believe you would develop. (Think Woody Allen and his imaginary brain tumor.)
- You often lose sleep worrying about what would happen to you if you lost a loved one, or what would happen to your loved ones if he or she lost you.
- You have trouble falling asleep because you can't slow down your frantic worrying process as you lie still in bed at night.
- When the phone rings or the mail arrives, you immediately imagine what kind of bad news you are about to receive.
- You feel compelled to control the behaviors of others because you worry that they can't take care of themselves.
- You are overly cautious about engaging in any behavior that could possible result in harm or hurt to you or to those around you, even if

the risk is small (such as driving a car, flying in an airplane, or visiting a big city).

If even just one of the worrywart characteristics describes you, you probably worry more than you have to. If most or all of these statements apply to you, worry is probably having a distinctly negative effect on you. Worry and the anxiety it can produce can cause specific physical, cognitive, and emotional symptoms, from heart palpitations, dry mouth, hyperventilation, muscle pain, and fatigue to fear, panic, anger, and depression. Worry is stressful.

## When Life Stinks: Chronic Stress

Chronic stress is much different from acute stress, although its long-term effects are much the same. Chronic stress has nothing to do with change. Chronic stress is long-term, constant, unrelenting stress on the body, mind, or spirit. For example, someone living in poverty for years and years is under chronic stress. So is someone with a chronic illness such as arthritis or migraine headaches or other conditions that result in constant pain. Living in a dysfunctional family or working at a job you hate is a source of chronic stress. So is deep-seated self-hatred or low self-esteem.

Some people's chronic stress is obvious. They live in horrible conditions or have to endure terrible abuse. They are in prison, live in a war-torn country, or are a minority in a place where minorities suffer constant discrimination. Other chronic stress is less obvious. The person who despises her job and feels she can never accomplish her dreams is under chronic stress. So is the person who feels stuck in a bad relationship.

### What are some ill effects of stress?

All forms of stress can result in a downward spiral of illness, depression, anxiety, and breakdown, physical, emotional, mental, and spiritual.

Sometimes, chronic stress is the result of acute or episodic stress. An acute illness can evolve into chronic pain. An abused child can grow up to suffer self-loathing or low self-esteem. The problem with chronic stress is that people become so used to it that they often can't begin to see how to get out of the situation. They come to believe life is supposed to be painful, stressful, or miserable.

Too much stress is dangerous. It saps the joy out of life. It can even kill, whether through a heart attack, a violent act, suicide, a stroke, or, as some research suggests, cancer.

## Stress on Your Body

You can control some of the stresses on your body; for example, you can determine how much you eat and how much you exercise. These stresses fall into the physiological stressor category. Then, there are environmental stressors, such as environmental pollution and substance addiction.

1. **Environmental stressors.** These are things in your immediate environment that put stress on your physical body. These include air pollution, polluted drinking water, noise pollution, artificial lighting, bad ventilation, or the presence of allergens in the field of ragweed outside your bedroom window or in

the dander of the cat who likes to sleep on your pillow.

2. **Physiological stressors.** These are the stressors within your own body that cause stress. For example, hormonal changes that occur during pregnancy or menopause put direct physiological stress on your system, as does premenstrual syndrome (PMS). Hormonal changes may also cause indirect stress because of the emotional changes they cause. Also, bad health habits such as smoking, drinking too much, eating junk food, or being sedentary put physiological stress on your body. So does illness, whether it's the common cold or something more serious like heart disease or cancer. Injury also puts stress on your body— a broken leg, a sprained wrist, and a slipped disk are all stressful.

Just as potent but less direct are stressors that impact your body by way of your mind. For example, getting caught in heavy traffic may stress your body directly because of the air pollution it creates, but it may also stress your body indirectly because you get so worked up and irritated sitting in your car in the middle of a traffic jam that your blood pressure rises, your muscles tense, and your heart beats faster. If you were to interpret the traffic jam differently—say, as an opportunity to relax and listen to your favorite CD before getting to work—your body might not experience any stress at all. Again, attitude plays a major role.

Pain is another, trickier example of indirect stress. If you have a terrible headache, your body may not experience direct physiological stress, but your emotional reaction to the pain might cause your body significant stress.

People tend to be fearful of pain, but pain is an important way to let us know something is wrong. Pain can signal injury or disease.

However, sometimes we already know what's wrong. We get migraines, or have arthritis, or experience menstrual cramps, or a bad knee acts up when the weather changes. This kind of "familiar" pain isn't useful in terms of alerting us to something that needs immediate medical attention.

But because we know we are in some form of pain, we still tend to get tense. "Oh no, not another migraine! No, not today!" Our emotional reaction doesn't cause the pain, but it does cause the physiological stress associated with the pain. Pain in itself isn't stressful. Our reaction to pain is what causes stress. So, learning stress management techniques may not stop pain, but it can stop the physiological stress associated with pain.

When your body is experiencing this stress response, whether caused by direct or indirect physiological stressors, it undergoes some very specific changes. Around the beginning of the twentieth century, physiologist Walter B. Cannon coined the phrase "fight or flight" to describe the biochemical changes stress invokes in the body, preparing it to flee or confront danger more safely and effectively. These are the changes that happen in your body every time you feel stressed, even if running away or fighting aren't relevant or wouldn't help you (for example, if you're about to give a speech, take a test, or confront your mother-in-law about her constant unsolicited advice, neither fight nor flight are very helpful responses).

Here's what happens inside your body when you feel stress:

1. Your cerebral cortex sends an alarm message to your hypothalamus, the part of your brain that releases the chemicals that create the stress response. Anything your brain perceives as stress will cause this effect, whether or not you are in any real danger.

2. Your hypothalamus releases chemicals that stimulate your sympathetic nervous system to prepare for danger.

3. Your nervous system reacts by raising your heart rate, respiration rate, and blood pressure. Everything gets turned "up."

4. Your muscles tense, preparing for action. Blood moves away from the extremities and your digestive system, into your muscles and brain. Blood sugars are mobilized to travel to where they will be needed most.

5. Your senses get sharper. You can hear better, see better, smell better, taste better. Even your sense of touch becomes more sensitive.

That sounds like a way to get things done, doesn't it? Imagine the high-powered executive, stunning clients with an on-target presentation and sharp, clever answers to every question. Imagine the basketball player at the championship game, making every shot. Imagine the student acing that final exam, every answer coming immediately to mind, the perfect words pouring from the pen for that A+ essay. Imagine yourself at the next office party, clever and funny, attracting crowds that hang on your every word.

Stress can cause problems in different systems all over your body. Some problems are immediate, like digestive trouble or a racing heartbeat. Other problems are more likely to occur the longer you are under stress.

But the downside is that stress, while beneficial in moderate amounts, is harmful in excessive amounts, as are most things. Some of stress's less desirable symptoms, directly related to the increase in adrenaline in the body, include the following:

- Sweating
- Cold extremities
- Nausea, vomiting, diarrhea
- Muscle tension
- Dry mouth
- Confusion

- Nervousness, anxiety
- Irritability, impatience
- Frustration
- Panic
- Hostility, aggression

Long-term effects of stress can be even harder to correct, and include such things as depression, loss or increase of appetite resulting in undesirable weight changes, frequent minor illnesses, increased aches and pains, sexual problems, fatigue, loss of interest in social activities, increased addictive behavior, chronic headaches, acne, chronic backaches, chronic stomachaches, and worsened symptoms associated with medical conditions such as asthma and arthritis.

# Chapter 2

# Breaking Down Stress

Now that you know what stress is, we can move closer to getting rid of it. First off, realize that no one is alone in the battle with stress—everyone is affected by it. Next, identify where your stress actually comes from, in order to remove unnecessary stressors so you can focus on the unavoidable ones. Then you can begin the battle to eliminate stress.

## Who Has It?

So, who is affected by all this stress? You? Your partner? Your parents? Your grandparents? Your kids? Your friends? Your enemies? The guy in the next cubicle? The woman in the elevator? The CEO? The people in the mailroom? Yes.

Almost everyone has experienced some kind of stress, and many people experience chronic stress, or constant, regular stress, every day of their lives.

Some people handle stress pretty well, even when it is extreme. Others fall apart under stress that seems negligible to the outside world. What's the difference? Some may have learned better coping mechanisms, but many researchers believe that people have an inherited level of stress tolerance. Some people can take a lot and still feel great and, in fact, do their best work under stress. Other people require very low-stress lives to function productively.

Nevertheless, we all experience stress some of the time, and these days, more and more people experience stress all of the time. The effects aren't just individualized, either. According to the American Institute of Stress in Yonkers, New York:

- An estimated 1 million people in the work force are absent on an average workday because of stress-related complaints.
- Nearly half of all American workers suffer from symptoms of burnout, or severe job-related stress that impairs or impedes functioning.
- Job stress costs U.S. industry $300 billion every year in absenteeism, diminished productivity, employee turnover, and direct medical, legal, and insurance fees.
- Between 60 percent and 80 percent of industrial accidents are probably due to stress.
- Workers' compensation awards for job stress, once rare, have become common. In California alone, employers paid almost $1 billion for medical and legal fees related to workers' compensation awards.
- Nine out of ten job stress suits are successful, with an average payout of more than four times the payout for injury claims.

Stress has become a way of life for many, but that doesn't mean we should sit back and accept the insidious effects of stress on our bodies, minds, and spirits. While you probably can't do much about the stress experienced by others (unless you're the cause of the stress), you can certainly tackle the stress in your own life (and that's a good way to stop being stressful to others!).

## Where Does It Come From?

Stress can come from inside. It can be caused by your perception of events, rather than by the events themselves. A job transfer might be a horrible stress to one person, a magnificent opportunity to another. A lot of stress depends on attitude.

But even when the stress is undeniably external—say, all your money was just embezzled—stress affects a host of changes inside your body. More specifically, stress in all its many forms interferes with the body's production of three very important hormones that help you feel balanced and "normal."

### *Serotonin*

Serotonin is the hormone that helps you get a good night's sleep. Produced in the pineal gland deep inside your brain, serotonin controls your body clock by converting into melatonin and then converting back into serotonin over the course of a twenty-four-hour day. This process regulates your energy, body temperature, and sleep cycle. The serotonin cycle synchronizes with the cycle of the sun, regulating itself according to exposure to daylight and darkness, which is why some people who are rarely exposed to the sun, such as those in northern climates, experience seasonal depression during the long, dark winter months—their serotonin production gets out of whack. Stress can throw it out of whack, too, and one result is the inability to sleep well. People under stress often experience a disturbed sleep cycle, manifesting itself as insomnia or an excessive need to sleep because the sleep isn't productive.

## *Noradrenaline*

A hormone produced by your adrenal glands, noradrenaline is related to the adrenaline that your body releases in times of stress to give you that extra chance at survival. Noradrenaline is related to your daily cycle of energy. Too much stress can disrupt your body's production of noradrenaline, leaving you with a profound lack of energy and motivation to do anything. It's that feeling you get when you just want to sit and stare at the television, even though you have a long list of things you absolutely have to do. If your noradrenaline production is disrupted, you'll probably just keep sitting there, watching television. You simply won't have the energy to get anything done.

## *Dopamine*

Dopamine is a hormone linked to the release of endorphin in your brain. Endorphin is that stuff that helps kill pain. Chemically, it is related to opiate substances like morphine and heroin, and, if you are injured, your body releases endorphin to help you function. When stress compromises your body's ability to produce dopamine, it also compromises your body's ability to produce endorphins, so you become more sensitive to pain. Dopamine is responsible for that wonderful feeling you get from doing things you enjoy. It makes you feel happy about life itself. Too much stress, too little dopamine, and nothing seems fun or pleasurable anymore. You feel flat. You feel depressed.

So, as you can see, stress comes from the inside as well as the outside. Your perception of events and the influences (such as health habits) on your body and mind actually cause chemical changes within your body. Anybody who ever doubted the intricate connection of the mind and body need only look at what happens when people feel stress and worry. It's all connected. (And therein lies a clue to what you can do about stress!)

## When Do You Get It?

Because there are so many forms of stress, stress can happen at any time. Stress is obvious when you experience a major life change, so expect stress when you move, lose someone you love, get married, change jobs, or experience a big change in financial status, diet, exercise habits, or health.

But you can also expect stress when you get a minor cold, have an argument with a friend, go on a diet, join a gym, stay out too late, drink too much, or even stay home with your kids all day when school is cancelled due to that irritating blizzard. Remember, stress often results from any kind of change in your normal routine. It also results from living a life that doesn't make you happy; if that is you, your whole life may be one long stress session. You need stress management now!

## Why, Why, Why?

Why stress? What's the point? Stress is a relatively complex interaction of external and internal processes caused by something relatively simple: the survival instinct. And that's important, even today!

Life is full of stimuli. We enjoy some of it. We don't enjoy some of it. But our bodies are programmed, through millions of years of learning how to survive, to react in certain ways to stimulus that is extreme. We've evolved so that if you should suddenly find yourself in a dangerous situation—you step in front of a speeding car, you lose your balance and teeter on the edge of a cliff, you call your boss a troglodyte when he is standing right behind you—your body will react in a way that will best ensure your survival. You might move extra fast. You might pitch yourself back to safety. You might think fast and talk your way out of trouble.

Whether you are being chased around the savanna by a hungry lion or around the parking lot by an aggressive car salesman, your body recognizes an alarm and pours stress hormones such as adrenaline and cortisol into your bloodstream. Adrenaline produces what scientists call the "fight or flight" response (which will be discussed further in the next chapter). It gives you an extra boost of strength and energy so that you can turn around and fight that lion, if you think you will win (you're probably better off pitted against the car salesman), or so that you can run like the dickens (also effective against car salesmen).

Adrenaline increases your heart rate and your breathing rate and sends blood straight to your vital organs so that they can work better—faster muscle response, quicker thinking, and so on. It also helps your blood to clot faster and draws blood away from your skin (if you should suffer a swipe of the lion's claw, you won't bleed as much) and also from your digestive tract (so you won't throw up—no, it doesn't always work). And cortisol flows through your body to keep the stress response responding as long as the stress continues.

Even back in the caveman days, people weren't being chased by hungry lions all day long, every day, for weeks on end (or, if they were, they really should have considered moving to a different cave).

Extreme physical reactions aren't meant to occur all the time. However, they are undeniably helpful during emergencies and other extreme situations.

Times that extreme physical reactions may aid you include fun situations like performing in a play or giving the toast at your best friend's wedding. The stress reaction can help you think more quickly, react more accurately, and respond with clever, witty repartee or just the right joke to keep the audience entranced by your sparkling performance.

But if you were to experience the constant release of adrenaline and cortisol every day, eventually the feeling would get tiresome, quite literally. You'd start to experience exhaustion, physical pain, a decrease in your ability to concentrate and remember, frustration, irritability, insomnia, possibly even violent episodes. Your body would become out of balance because we aren't designed to be under stress all the time.

But these days, life moves so quickly, technology allows us to do ten times more in a fraction of the time, and everybody wants everything yesterday, so stress happens. But too much stress will negate the effects of all that great technology—you won't get any work done if you have no energy, no motivation, and keep getting sick.

## So, How Do You Get Rid of It?

You may not feel like the stress in your life is quite so bad just yet. You aren't on the verge of a heart attack or a nervous breakdown . . . are you?

But what will happen if you don't begin to manage your stress right now? How long will you allow stress to compromise your quality of life, especially knowing you don't have to let it? That's where stress management comes in, and stress management is the focus of this book.

> As pervasive as stress may be in all its forms, stress management techniques that really work are equally pervasive.

You can manage, even eliminate, the negative stress in your life. All you have to do is find the stress management techniques that work best for you. Learn them and turn your life around.

And that's the point of this book. You'll learn all about stress management in its many forms so that you can design a stress management program that works for you.

# Chapter 3

# Building a Stress-Proof Body

Now it's time to start learning
strategies to combat stress. In
this chapter, we'll cover some
of the most basic things you
can do to start relieving your
stress today. You'll learn some
easy strategies that will set the
groundwork for a body and
a mind that can handle the
necessary stresses of life.

## Stress Management Strategies: Sleep

If you commit to getting a good night's sleep, you'll find your stress management reserves growing. Here are some tips to get you started on the road to eight quality hours of sleep each night:

- **Figure out why you aren't getting enough sleep, then commit to changing your routine.** Where are you wasting time during the day? How could you rearrange your schedule to get some things done earlier, allowing for an earlier bedtime? Could you rearrange your schedule to allow a later wake-up time? If you are staying up late to watch TV or surf the Internet, try skipping the media blitz for a few nights to see how the extra sleep changes your mood and energy level.
- **Create a bedtime ritual for yourself. Parents are often advised to give their sleep-resistant children a routine, but the technique works for grownups, too.** Your routine should include a series of steps that are conducive to relaxation—for example, a bath or shower, then perhaps a few minutes of deep breathing or other relaxation

technique; a cup of herbal tea; a good book instead of the television or computer; swapping back rubs, neck rubs, or foot rubs with a partner; writing in your journal. Then, it's lights out.

- **Try not to get into the habit of falling asleep in front of the TV.** Once in the habit, falling asleep without the TV will probably take longer, and you may not sleep as well. If this happens, try some relaxation techniques.

- **If you feel you are wasting precious time by sleeping when you should be getting things done, keep reminding yourself that sleep is getting things done.** While you sleep, your body is busy healing, recharging by conserving energy, growing and regenerating cells, and consolidating memory and discharging emotions through dreams. You're actually being pretty productive when you sleep, and you'll be even more productive after you've had a good sleep.

- **Don't get all stressed out about not being able to get to sleep.** An occasional night of too-few ZZZs won't hurt you as long as you usually get enough sleep. Rather than lying in the dark, tossing and turning in frustration, turn on the light and find something to read.

Get comfortable. Sip some warm milk or chamomile tea. Meditate. Steer your mind away from worries and think about pleasant things—not sleep, just pleasant things. Breathe. Even if you don't get to sleep, at least you'll get to relax. And you'll probably feel drowsy soon.

### If you are having trouble sleeping, try these suggestions:

- **Don't drink or eat anything with caffeine after lunch if you are having problems getting to sleep.** That includes coffee, tea, cola, and many other sodas (check the label); certain over-the-counter pain medications and cold medications (check the label); stimulants designed to keep you awake; and even cocoa and chocolate.
- **Eat a healthy, light, low-fat, low-carbohydrate dinner.** Fresh fruits and vegetables, whole grains instead of refined grains, and low-fat protein like fish, chicken, beans, and tofu will help your body to be in a calmer, more balanced state come bedtime. Avoid high-fat, overly processed foods in the evening. You'll

be more likely to suffer digestive problems that can keep you from sleeping. (You know the feeling—getting up at 3:00 A.M. in a desperate attempt to find those Tums . . . )

- **Eat a light dinner.** Late, large dinners are upsetting to your digestive system. For a peaceful night's sleep, make dinner your lightest meal.

- **For an evening snack, eat foods high in tryptophan, an amino acid that encourages the body to produce serotonin, a chemical that helps you to sleep.** Serotonin also regulates your moods, helping you to feel good. Foods high in tryptophan include milk, turkey, peanut butter, rice, tuna, dates, figs, and yogurt. A light snack about thirty to sixty minutes before bedtime that includes any of these foods can help promote restful sleep.

- **Don't drink alcohol in the evening.** While many people have a drink thinking it will help them get to sleep, alcohol actually disrupts sleep patterns, making your sleep less restful. Alcohol may also increase snoring and sleep apnea.

- **Get enough exercise during the day.** A well-exercised body will fall asleep faster, sleep longer, and sleep more productively.
- **If you are still having problems sleeping, talk to your doctor about it.** Studies show that two thirds of Americans have never been asked by their doctors how well they sleep, but 80 percent have never brought up the subject with their doctors, either. Tell your doctor you are concerned about your sleep problems. He or she may have a simple solution.

## Stress Management Strategies: Hydration

Sometimes, one of the most helpful things you can do for your body when you're feeling anxious is to have a drink of water. Human bodies are about two-thirds water, but many people are mildly dehydrated (3 percent to 5 percent below their body weight due to fluid loss) and don't know it.

While severe dehydration (10 percent or more fluid loss) has dramatic symptoms and can even result in death, mild dehydration may go unnoticed and is more likely to occur after intense exercise, in extreme heat, while dieting, and after vomiting or diarrhea, either from illness or as a result of food poisoning or drinking too much alcohol.

**What does dehydration have to do with stress?**

When you are walking around without enough water in your body, your body will experience stress, and you'll be less equipped to handle stress from other sources.

Symptoms of dehydration include the following:

- Dry mouth
- Dizziness
- Light-headedness
- Dark urine (should be pale yellow)
- Inability to concentrate
- Confusion

One reason people tend to be so often dehydrated is that caffeinated beverages are so popular and widely available. While you feel like your thirst is being quenched when you drink a can of cola, the caffeine is actually acting as a diuretic to flush water out of your system.

Yet, water can offer your body many benefits that caffeinated beverages can't, not the least of which is a stronger defense against stress. If you are dehydrated—according to the statistics, you very well may be—your body can't rally its energy in the cause of stress management because it is too busy trying to compensate for its lack of water.

> Drinking more water is one of the easiest changes you can make to help manage your stress.

With a well-hydrated body, you'll feel better. Your skin will look better. You'll have more energy. So, drink up!

Like anything else, drinking water is a habit. If you don't get into the habit, you'll drink water for a few days then go back to your five-cans-of-diet-soda-per-day habit. Here are some tips to get into this healthful habit:

- **If you really don't like the taste of plain water, try a few brands of mineral-added bottled water.** The minerals give the water more flavor. Or, add a wedge of lemon, lime, or orange to your water. If you just have to have those bubbles, try club soda instead of soda. Still not charmed? Dilute real fruit juice (not the sugar-added stuff) with half water or half club soda.

- **Ideally, you should drink sixty-four ounces, or eight cups, of water each day.** That sounds like a lot, but if you space it throughout the day, it's not so much. Have sixteen ounces first thing in the morning, sixteen ounces with lunch, sixteen ounces with dinner, and sixteen ounces in the evening. Add another sixteen ounces or more if you've been sweating or getting a lot of exercise.

- **We have become so removed from our natural sensations of hunger that we often mistake thirst for hunger and eat when all we really need is a tall cool glass of $H_2O$.** A glass of water before each meal and whenever hunger pangs strike between meals should satisfy your body's need for water and help to curb excessive eating.

## Get a Handle on Bad Habits

Bad habits can be irritating, to ourselves or others, but they can also be stressful. Many bad habits undermine physical health, emotional well-being, and mental acuity. To begin building a body capable of managing the stresses that life necessarily entails, get control over your bad habits; they are the stresses that aren't necessary. Habits are stressful in the following three ways.

### Direct

Many habits have a direct, negative effect on the body. Smoking, drinking too much alcohol, and taking certain drugs (legal or illegal) can introduce toxic or harmful substances into the body that can compromise the body's ability to function properly, lead to addiction, even encourage disease processes. Habits can also directly impact our emotional or mental functioning. Becoming intoxicated, overly distracted, or otherwise impaired can make one more prone to accidents, rages, and mistakes. When your body and/or mind are directly affected in a negative way by a habit, your stress level will increase.

### Indirect

Habits also have an indirect effect on your stress level. Knowing you drank too much, stayed up too late, and ate too much the night before can add to your frustration and low self-esteem in your work life the next morning. Your stress will be higher than it would have been had you not spent the evening before being controlled by a bad habit. Maybe someone will comment on your ragged nails and make you feel embarrassed and angry at yourself. Later, you might snap at a friend because you feel bad about your lack of control. Habits can make us feel helpless when they control us, causing stress because we worry about our lack of self-control, the effect our habit may have on others, and the deleterious health effects of whatever the habit may be.

### *Combination*

Some habits can have both direct and indirect negative effects. Probably most bad habits fall into this category. After all, anything that affects us negatively and that we could have controlled but didn't will tend to undermine our emotional state and self-esteem, leading to related stress. Compulsive overeating, for example, is dangerous to the body because the body isn't designed to take in huge amounts of food at one time. It can also create negative emotional states such as frustration, depression, and anxiety. Even less dramatic bad habits like habitual messiness can have a combination effect. If you can never keep things clean, for example, you might suffer frustration over never being able to find things, financial loss because of disorganization, and low self-esteem because it seems like everyone else is able to keep things neat but you (which, of course, is not true).

Some habits, of course, are good. If you always clean up your own messes, have a habit of being polite, or are devoted to your daily bowl of fresh salad, you probably already know that those habits are keepers.

Some habits are neutral. For example, you always eat a favorite cereal, or you prefer a certain gas station, or you have a habit of humming while you wash the dishes. If they don't bother anybody, no problem.

Other habits aren't so good. What makes a habit bad? A bad habit is a habit that makes you less healthy or less happy.

Even if you feel good while indulging your bad habit, you probably know when it's just a temporary high.

When you indulge in something empty like when you go to the mall and spend $400 on stuff you don't really need, you get a rush, but as soon as you get home and put the things away, you begin to feel guilt, regret, or even anger at yourself. The habit was controlling you rather than the other way around.

You may feel helpless in the throes of your nail biting, hair twirling, chip munching, TV watching, or procrastinating habit. But as helpless as you feel, rest assured that it's a habit, and habits can be broken. How do you break a bad habit? First, determine if your habit really is bad. If, for example, you drink a cup of coffee every morning because you really enjoy it, that's probably fine. If your habit controls you—if you gulp down java by the quart all day long and feel panicky or nonfunctional without it, you've got a bad habit.

## Stress Management Strategies: Reshaping Bad Habits

Knowing you need to change things can be overwhelming, but having some specific strategies can help you to set goals and work on things one step at a time. Use the following list as a guideline to help you set goals. Try one strategy each week, and don't get frustrated. You've had that habit for a long time, and it may take awhile to retrain yourself, but you can do it!

### Practice the Pause

Know your habit, and when you are about to fall into your habitual behavior, learn to pause, just for a moment, and think. Ask yourself these questions: Will this nourish my body? Will this nourish my spirit? Is this good for me? Will I feel good about doing this later? Or, will I feel guilty about it later? Is it worth the momentary pleasure? Is it really worth the momentary pleasure?

### Don't Have Habit Triggers in Your House

If sugar sets you off on a binge, don't keep sugary snacks around. If you can't resist shopping, don't keep your credit card in your wallet when you know you have to go to the mall, or better yet, leave your credit card at home. Bring just enough cash to make your purchase, and no more. Don't keep alcohol in the house if that's your weakness. If nighttime television is your weakness, get that TV out of your bedroom. Put it in the kitchen to make cleaning more interesting, or even (gulp) pack it away.

### Replace the Habit

If you use your bad habit to soothe your stress, replace your habit (food, cigarettes, excessive Internet surfing) with another kind of "treat" that is just as good or better. Make that "treat" easily accessible in situations where you know you'll be tempted to lapse into your habit. For example, if you automatically turn on the television as soon as you get home from work, allow yourself twenty minutes of quiet time instead. Don't let anyone disturb you! Put on relaxing music and breathe, meditate, have some tea, read a book, peruse a magazine, or just take a catnap. You'll be recharged far beyond what that hour of soap operas or tell-all talk shows could have done.

### Make a Specialty

Turn your habit into your specialty by becoming a connoisseur! Let food become a genuine pleasure. Focus on quality, not quantity. If you want food, eat a small amount of something really good. Savor every bite. Never waste your time, energy, or health on large amounts of substandard food. The same goes for alcohol. Rather than drinking as much as you can of whatever is available, settle for only small amounts of the very best. And the same goes for shopping. Don't just buy whatever you see. Collect something valuable and learn all about it. For example, learn about early American ceramics or antique train sets or Victorian hat pins or dog statues from around the world—whatever strikes you as interesting.

If you love to watch television, watch only quality television. Become an expert on classic movies or independent films. Watch and learn from nature shows, or science shows, or shows about art, cooking, whatever you like. You might even learn how to make your own movies. If you can't do without noise, learn all about classical music or jazz or classic rock or whatever you like.

Becoming a connoisseur doesn't work for every habit, of course. One can't really become a connoisseur of procrastination, for example. But a little creativity can still transform any habit into a hobby or even a specialty.

Or, you can throw yourself into the reverse of your habit. A nail biter? Learn how to do manicures and pedicures. A slob? Become an expert at organizing your household and routines in a way that minimizes cleaning. Many self-professed slobs have reformed and created successful careers for themselves as professional organizers. Quitting your old, harmful habit may result in a healthy and beneficial new habit.

# Chapter 4

# Get Strong, Get Healthy

If you've ever tried to lose weight, you've heard the mantra, "Eat less, exercise more." The same prescription can help to decrease the effects of stress in your life. Exercise builds muscle, increases lung capacity, improves cardiovascular function, and triggers the release of chemicals that counteract the effects of stress.

## Move It or Lose It!

Exercise may be one of the most perfect stress management tools, yet it's often the first thing to go when our schedules get too busy. Because there is no "deadline" associated with daily exercise, it's easy to bump exercise to the bottom of the priority list.

Or, is there a deadline?

Many researchers believe that poor health habits—most essentially, lack of exercise, improper diet, and smoking—are responsible for a significant proportion of deaths from heart disease and cancer. Are we fast approaching our "deadline" without having established good health habits? Maybe it would be wise to move it so that we don't lose it.

According to the Centers for Disease Control and Prevention (CDC), Americans are no more fit than they were in 1990. Now, as then, only about 25 percent of American adults get enough exercise to achieve health benefits.

### *The Body's Reaction*

Moderate exercise, according to an increasing number of experts, may be the single most effective way to get stress under control. Are we sabotaging our own stress management efforts because we think we're too busy to get up and take a walk? We certainly aren't helping our body deal with the effects of stress by leading a sedentary life. Why?

I've told you how stress evokes the "fight or flight" reaction by releasing stress hormones into the body designed to give us sudden, quick reactions, extra strength, and endurance. When we don't respond to the stress response by moving quickly, using our strength, or taking advantage of the added endurance, our bodies are all geared up with no outlet for that energy. Muscles stay tense. Blood pressure stays high. Breathing stays shallow. Cortisol and adrenaline course through the body causing all kinds of problems when the body doesn't react the way it is being programmed to react.

Exercise changes the picture, accomplishing two important things in the wake of the stress response:

1. **Exercise allows the body to expend energy** so that while your brisk walk around the block may not actually be "fight or flight," to the body, the message is the same. That extra energy available to your body is being used, signaling the body that it can, after exercise, return to equilibrium.

2. **Exercise also releases chemicals like beta endorphins that specifically counteract the effects of stress hormones,** alerting the body that the danger has passed and the relaxation response can begin.

In other words, exercise makes the obsolete "fight or flight" stress response relevant again. It lets your body respond the way it is trying to respond. Rather than sitting and fuming (what caveperson ever did that in response to a charging predator?), you are getting up and moving. "Ahh . . ." the body responds. "Ahh, this is what I want to do!"

But making yourself get up and exercise is the trick. While I don't mean to beat a dead caveperson, our prehistoric ancestors didn't have much of a choice: It was exercise or die.

### *Getting into the Habit*

Some of think we can get along just fine, thank you, without moving very much at all. We might move from room to room in the house, or from house to car to office desk to car to house, but that's relatively insignificant compared to the kind of day-to-day, hardworking, on-the-move kind of existence humans once knew.

Exercising enough is certainly possible, however, in modern life. Resources are widely available to help, making exercise easy to accomplish for those who really want to accomplish it. For some people, exercise is already a good habit, or a priority to keep energy high and weight under control. For others, exercising is akin to having a root canal. They don't like it, they don't want to do it, and they see absolutely no good reason to break a sweat.

Most of us are probably somewhere in between. We know exercise is good for us and we do it . . . occasionally—when the mood strikes or time permits. The trouble is, exercising in fits and starts isn't enough to accomplish long-term stress management or a decreased risk of developing chronic illness.

### *Getting Motivated*

Since you aren't compelled, you need to be motivated. When life is busy and full, forcing yourself to spend thirty minutes daily doing something you hate when nobody is making you do it . . . well, you do the math. It's not going to happen.

However, even if you are a die-hard exercise hater, you can probably find something you like. Maybe your idea of exercise is an aerobics class, but you can't stand the pressure of standing in the midst of all those young, fit, barely-twenty year olds. Maybe you're one of those twenty year olds, but you can't seem to master the fancy footwork. Or, maybe you think exercise is jogging or team sports or calisthenics, and you'd rather eat worms.

**How do I get in the regular habit of exercising?**

The trick is finding an exercise plan you can stick with—one that holds your interest, works with your lifestyle, and is safe for your body type (always check with your doctor before starting an exercise regimen).

Whatever your preconception, fear not. Exercise is a broad term. Just about anybody can find some kind of exercise they actually enjoy. Maybe joining a gym is the answer for you—all those classes, all that equipment, the sauna and spa to relax you afterward, even child care! Maybe you need something more tranquil than high-impact aerobics, and you'll find new inspiration in a yoga class. Maybe you just need to get out into the fresh air and take a walk. What could be easier?

Even if you find something you can only, at best, tolerate, try it for a while. Expand your fitness horizons and keep an open mind.

Try one type of exercise, then try another, then another until you find something you like enough to stick with. You'll accumulate a lot more hours of exercise than if you just sit there rejecting the prospect. Once you begin to experience the stress-relieving benefits of regular exercise, that daily trip to the gym or that yoga class may seem a lot more attractive, even an essential part of your day. You might even learn to like it!

## The Whole-Body Effects of Exercise

You've heard exercise is good for you. You even feel better after you do it, so you know it's doing something good. But what does it do, exactly, and how can it help relieve stress? Exercise benefits the body in very specific ways. Here are some of the benefits of moderate exercise:

- Stronger muscles
- Better flexibility
- Increased heart and lung efficiency
- Decreased risk of developing heart disease
- Decreased risk of developing lung disease
- Improved overall circulation
- Reduced cholesterol levels
- Reduced blood pressure
- Strengthened immune system
- Decrease in excess body fat
- Increased energy
- Decreased symptoms of depression
- Decreased symptoms of arthritis
- Decreased risk of diabetes and decreased risk of complications from diabetes
- Decreased risk of osteoporosis and decreased risk of complications from osteoporosis

- Improved quality of sleep and decrease in insomnia
- Increased mental acuity
- Improved posture
- Improved self-image
- Decreased frequency of injuries in daily life
- Decreased effects of stress
- Improved ability to manage stress

Not only does exercise help the body to deal with the physical effects of stress, but it helps the mind to feel more in control and able to manage stress. Add to that the positive effect exercise has on so many other disorders and its ability to help prevent so many physical problems, and you've got a stress management tool that is both preventive and proactive.

## Finding a Movement Plan You Can Live With

So many types of exercise, so little time! Of course, not all of the types of exercise in the following sections will appeal to you, but maybe you'll get some new ideas. Here are brief descriptions of some of the more common types of exercise. Don't be afraid to try something new, especially if you feel like you are in an exercise rut or need inspiration to get you started.

If you are very overweight, have a health problem, or haven't exercised in over six months, please consult your doctor before beginning any exercise program. Exercise is one of the most recommended ways to battle stress.

### Walking

Walking is great. It's easy, fun, and can get you out in the fresh air or can provide an opportunity for socializing with friends while you all shape up together. Walk at a brisk pace for thirty to sixty minutes at least three times each week, and preferably five to six times per week.

### Swimming

Swimming is great for people who love the water, people with joint or orthopedic problems, and people who have a lot of weight to lose. The water buoys the body so that joints, bones, and muscles don't feel the impact of exercise, making injuries less likely for people who are vulnerable to the impact. Work up gradually to thirty to sixty minutes of steady swimming. Varying your strokes—freestyle, breaststroke, backstroke, and sidestroke—will help work all your muscles.

### Join a Gym

For some people, joining a gym is the inspiration they needed all along. A gym provides fellowship, a wide range of fitness possibilities from aerobics classes (step aerobics, cardio funk, kickboxing, and many other types of aerobics are offered these days) to yoga to racquetball to swimming to weight lifting to the latest in exercise machines, from high-tech treadmills to no-impact elliptical trainers. In many clubs, you can also find personal trainers, nutritionists, sports leagues, and child care, as well as other amenities such as massage therapists, saunas, spas, steam rooms, and snack bars filled with healthy fare.

Plus, if you've paid for a membership, you might be more inspired to get your money's worth. Going to the gym can be a mini-break, a special treat, something you look forward to every day.

## *Yoga*

Yoga is an ancient Indian method of exercise designed to "yoke" body and mind. Yoga involves specific postures, breathing exercise, and meditation. Hatha Yoga, most popular in the West, consists primarily of the postures and breathing exercises.

Yoga is an excellent fitness activity on its own and also makes the perfect complement to other fitness activities because it increases strength, flexibility, circulation, posture, and overall body condition. Yoga is great both for people who have a hard time slowing down (you'll learn how great it feels and how important it is to move your body with slow control) and for people who have a hard time engaging in high-impact or fast-paced exercise (yoga is adaptable to all fitness levels and it's decidedly low impact).

Yoga is among the more perfect stress management exercises. Its original purpose was to gain control over the body and bring it into a state of balance in order to free the mind for spiritual contemplation. Yoga can help you to master your body so that it doesn't master you.

### The Great Outdoors

If you feel particularly inspired by great views, fresh air, and the lovely and varied smells of the natural world, choosing an outdoor exercise can inspire you to keep up the habit. Whether you walk, jog, run, bicycle, roller blade, cross-country ski, hike, or climb mountains, exercising outdoors is good for your body and soul. And who says you can't take a walk in the rain or the snow? Exercising outside, even for just a little while each day, can also help to keep you in touch with the natural world, which helps to put things in perspective—and that all on its own can relieve a lot of stress!

### Dance

Whether you take an organized class—ballet, jazz, tap, ballroom dancing, swing dancing, country dancing, square dancing, Irish step-dancing, to name a few—or go out dancing with your friends every weekend, dancing is great cardiovascular exercise and also a lot of fun. Something about music makes exercise seem less like exercise, and dancing, especially for fun, even alone in your house with the music blaring, is about as "unexercise-like" as you can get, but with all the benefits. Vigorous dancing can also be an excellent way to relieve tension and anxiety. So, get up and shake it!

### Team Sports

For people who like to play on a team and are motivated and energized by the energy of others, team sports can be an excellent way to get exercise and a social life at the same time. Weekend football games, tennis leagues, racquetball tournaments, playground basketball games, beach volleyball, or whatever else is available in your area and interesting to you can be so much fun that you'll forget you're exercising!

### *Massage Therapy*

Massage is an excellent stress management tool. It helps your body and mind to relax as it encourages the body to help heal itself. Massage can also give you a feeling of control and mastery over your body as it responds to the targeted effects of massage. Pain may disappear. Posture may improve. Muscles and joints may begin to work better and more easily. Massage also feels great and shouldn't be relegated to the status of occasional indulgence. Consider regular massage as a serious stress management tool. Massage can equal mental and physical maintenance.

Massage therapists are trained to knead and manipulate the muscles and connective tissue in the body to help the body find its equilibrium after exercise. Regular massage is great even for nonexercisers. It activates muscles and skin, improving circulation and even organ function. Your doctor may be able to refer you to a professional massage therapist, and, in some cases, massage therapy and even acupuncture is covered by insurance. If you are interested in less mainstream types of massage therapy such as reflexology, acupressure, or Reiki, talk to friends, a natural health provider, a yoga teacher, or the employees at your local natural health food store for recommendations. Some areas have directories of natural health care providers. Here are some of the common types of massage.

### Shiatsu and Acupressure

Shiatsu is the Japanese word for "finger pressure" and is sometimes known as acupressure. Shiatsu is an ancient form of massage, still widely practiced, that involves the application of pressure through fingers, palms, elbows, or knees to pressure points in the body. Pressure points are certain points along energy meridians that the Japanese and other Asian cultures have defined within the body. Pressure on these points is thought to release energy blockages that cause pain and disease, resulting in balance, equilibrium, and greater physical health. Acupuncture is based on the same principle but uses very thin needles painlessly inserted into pressure points. Although the idea may sound strange to a

Westerner, much research has supported the effectiveness of both acupuncture and acupressure in the relief of pain and the treatment of certain disorders.

### Reflexology

Reflexology is a little like acupressure, but in reflexology, all the pressure points are in the hands and feet. The theory goes that the entire body, including all the parts, organs, and glands, is represented in a "map" on the hands and feet, and that pressure applied to the right area of the "map" will help to balance the problem in the associated area of the body. Knowing the map allows people to work on themselves by rubbing their own hands or feet in the appropriate area.

### Variety Is the Spice of Exercise

No matter what types of exercise you choose, you'll work a wider range of muscles and reap a wider range of benefits if you vary your exercise. Try a different kind of activity once a week.

Also, varying your pace can add up to increased health benefits. Author and exercise physiologist Greg Landry, M.S., suggests interval training, a simple way to vary any exercise you're already doing. Landry suggests warming up for five minutes, then exercising at your regular pace for four minutes, then stepping up the pace for one minute. Then, for the rest of your workout, work four minutes at a regular pace, then one minute at a fast pace, and so forth. Interval training can help you to break past a weight loss plateau, help get you in shape faster, increase your energy and your body's rate of calorie burning by raising your base metabolism rate, and keep your workout more interesting. Changing pace every five minutes may also help to keep you more focused on your workout, too, which is a nice break for your busy brain.

# Chapter 5

# Diet and Nutrition

Stressed or not, you have to eat. But what will you choose to eat? Americans are notorious for making less than ideal dietary choices. Whether you are cursed with a sweet tooth or a penchant for pepperoni pizza, stress can make you less likely to keep compulsive eating under control.

## Fueling Up: The Stress Connection

Stress-related eating may be particularly dangerous to your health. In a recent ABC news special on stress, one segment was devoted to recent research that reveals the difference between "regular fat" and "stress fat." Stress fat, the segment explained, is not the lumpy, bumpy stuff you can see jiggling on your thighs and upper arms. Stress fat is the fat that accumulates deep inside the body, specifically around the internal organs of your torso.

This "stress fat" is the only fat that is known to contribute to heart disease, cancer, and diabetes. The only kind! And you can't even see it. This dangerous fat may be directly related to stress (among other things, including estrogen levels). Research shows that compulsive eating related to stress is more likely to result in fat accumulation around the internal organs.

Other studies suggest that while cortisol is a powerful appetite stimulant and can trigger excessive eating in the stressed-out among us, cortisol may actually encourage the body to accumulate fat in the abdominal region, especially in "apple-shaped" women—women who tend to gain weight around the middle rather than in the buttocks and legs (the so-called pear shape).

Stress-related eating is the beginning of a vicious circle. You feel stressed, so you eat foods that are likely to increase your susceptibility to stress. Consequently, you feel more stressed and eat more of those same stress-promoting foods.

Knowledge is power, and although knowledge may not equal willpower, it is the first step. Certain foods are known to have a disruptive effect on the body's equilibrium, while other foods are known to have a more balancing effect. Many cultures have discovered this food/body connection. Ayurveda, an ancient Indian system of health maintenance and improvement still popular today, focuses on balancing the body through food as well as other practices. Many contemporary researchers and health promoters also emphasize the link between good health, balance, energy, and the food we eat.

## Vitamins, Minerals, and More

Another way to build a healthy body that is best able to combat excessive stress is to make sure you aren't suffering from any basic deficiencies in vitamins, minerals, and phytochemicals (substances in plants thought to improve health and strengthen the immune system). While not everyone agrees that supplements are important, most of us don't get a chance to eat a completely balanced, well-rounded diet every single day. So, think of a supplement as an insurance policy. For your best nutritional defense against stress, follow these guidelines:

- **Eat a balanced diet.**
- If your doctor says it's OK, **take a multivitamin/ multimineral tablet every day** to strengthen your reserves and cover your nutritional bases.
- **Vitamins C, E, beta carotene (a form of vitamin A), selenium, and zinc are antioxidants.** Studies suggest extra antioxidants in the diet can reduce the risk of heart attack, stroke, and cataracts and can slow the aging process. (Note: Antioxidant supplements have been shown to increase the risk of cancer in smokers.)

Antioxidants from citrus fruits; broccoli; tomatoes; leafy greens; dark orange, yellow, and red vegetables; nuts; seeds; and vegetable oils are always good for you.

- **The B vitamins are great in many ways.** Many of them are thought to boost immunity, improve skin quality, protect against cancer, help arthritis symptoms, help the body to metabolize food and produce energy, and even help to reduce the effects of stress in the body.

- **Calcium** is a mineral that is essential for maintaining bone mass, preventing cancer and heart disease, reducing blood pressure, treating arthritis, promoting sleep, metabolizing iron, and reducing PMS symptoms.

- **Many other trace minerals keep the body healthy and working correctly,** from copper and chromium to iron and iodine to selenium, vanadium, and zinc.

- **Amino acids and essential fatty acids** are also necessary for a healthy functioning body.

- **Read about supplements if it interests you.** Much is made of other "supplement-of-the-week" substances. There may be something to some of these claims. Others may later prove false.

But remember, the most important thing is to eat a healthy, balanced, varied diet.

## Herbal Stress Remedies

Herbalism is an ancient and time-tested art that remains alive and well today. Many people take herbal remedies, from the popular echinacea for colds to more complex preparations for every imaginable ailment. A good herbalist can help you treat your health problems naturally and can be an excellent complement to conventional medicine.

Herbal remedies can be infused into water for teas, decoctions, and infusions; syrup, to make herbs more palatable; alcohol for tinctures; oil, to rub into skin; they can be mixed with cream, for external application; they can be formed into tablets or put inside capsules for easy swallowing; or they can even be put into the bath.

Although you can buy many herbs at your local pharmacy or even at the grocery store, herbs aren't FDA regulated, so your best bet is to go to an accredited herbalist with a good reputation.

Herbalists know about the side effects of different herbs and also how they interact with other medications. To find an herbalist, look in the phone book, ask the employees at your local health food store, or talk to friends for a referral. Some areas have directories of natural health care providers.

While many prescription medications are made from or derived from herbs, herbalists use herbal prescriptions to treat the whole person, not just an isolated condition. Herbalists believe that medical treatment should involve the least possible intervention and should strengthen the body's healing powers.

## Diets

It's easy to find fad diets that promise miraculous results, and it's equally easy to find people to proclaim how this or that diet was the only thing that worked for them. Many of these diets are controversial. Some people swear by the diet that suggests different blood types should focus on different foods. Others are devoted to the low-carb diets such as the Zone Diet, the Atkins Diet, the Protein Power diet, and the Carbohydrate Addict's diet. Some people choose a vegetarian or vegan (no animal products at all including dairy and eggs) diet. There are countless others.

Maybe one of these diets will work for you—check with your doctor. They all make interesting points and include healthy eating plans (not everybody agrees they are all healthy, but then again, not everybody agrees on anything).

The blood-type diets are all low in calories and high in natural, minimally processed foods. The low-carb diets make a good point: Refined carbohydrates tend to spike insulin levels, and in some people, insulin fluctuations seem to cause food binges and unusual weight gain. For the last few decades, the common wisdom has been "carbs, carbs, and more carbs." Now, the low-carb diets suggest that we need to get more protein back into our lives, and for some people, it's the answer to carbohydrate binges and can put a stop to massive weight gain.

Vegetarian and vegan diets have merit, too. Animal products have been associated with an increased risk of certain diseases, and many available animal products, from rich cheeses to marbled meats to the preservative-infused lunch meats we feed to our children, are high in saturated fat, calories, and, in the case of the cured meats, salt and preservatives, some of which are known carcinogens. Vegetarians tend to eat more vegetables, fruit, whole grains, beans, nuts, and seeds, and other healthy, unprocessed foods. That's certainly an improvement over lunch at the fast-food drive through (although more fast-food restaurants are serving healthier fare, by popular demand).

## General Nutrition Tips

If all the diets out there baffle you, you can feel comforted. They all boil down to a few simple rules that, when applied, will help just about anybody to reach and maintain a healthy weight, feel energized, and manage stress from a dietary perspective:

- **Whenever possible, eat food as close to its natural state as you can.** Eat an orange instead of drinking orange juice, but drink orange juice instead of orange soda. Eat a broiled, free-range, organic chicken breast instead of a minced, shaped, breaded, fried chicken patty. Choose brown rice over white, old-fashioned oats over instant flavored oatmeal, instant oatmeal over a toaster pastry. Eat whole wheat bread or, better yet, sprouted wheat bread instead of plain white bread, and spread it with natural, organic peanut or almond butter.

- **Choose nutrient-dense foods instead of foods that are mostly empty calories.** For example, dried fruit is more nutrient-dense than candy, broccoli and carrots with yogurt dip are more nutrient-dense than chips or popcorn, and freshly squeezed fruit or vegetable juice is more nutrient dense than soda. Less nutrient-dense food can be useful to help fill you up if it is low in calories and you are trying to lose weight (popcorn, for example, can help stave off hunger pangs, as long as you don't pour butter all over it).

- **Start and end the day with protein and complex carbohydrates** rather than simple carbohydrates such as sugar.

- **Eat a hearty breakfast, a moderate lunch, and a light dinner,** or, if you aren't a breakfast person, a light breakfast, a hearty lunch, and a light dinner.
- **Stop before you are stuffed** and don't eat more calories than you need.
- **Don't let more than about 30 percent of your calories come from fat,** and try to eat fat mostly from sources that contain a higher proportion of monounsaturated fat (olive oil, canola oil, avocados, walnuts, and walnut oil) and omega-3 fatty acids (in fatty fish like salmon and tuna), rather than saturated fat (meat and dairy products), trans-fatty acids (in margarine, vegetable shortening, and partially hydrogenated oils), and polyunsaturated fats (prevalent in many vegetable oils).

## Rethinking the "Treat"

Some people eat pretty well some of the time but can't get over the notion that on special occasions or when they've had a hard day (and lately, most of them have seemed pretty hard), they deserve a treat. If you are one of those people, you can rethink the "treat" concept.

It is so easy to eat in response to stress. Many people do it. After all, don't you deserve it? Don't you deserve a treat?

A little bit of something superb is a far more rewarding and sensual experience than a whole huge bunch of low-quality anything.

Sure you do. But a treat doesn't have to be about food. A treat could be a movie, a day trip, a full hour of doing nothing, a visit to the salon, a game of golf in the middle of the afternoon on a Wednesday, letting yourself go to bed at 9:00 P.M. There is so much that is wonderful, fun, and rewarding in life that has nothing to do with food. So, get in the habit of thinking creatively about how to reward yourself.

And if you just have to reward yourself with food, make it absolutely worth the indulgence.

A single piece of the highest quality imported chocolate, a thin slice of cake and a tiny cup of espresso from the best dessert café in town, a small but perfect filet mignon wrapped in the best bacon, or whatever your indulgence—savor every bite and don't do anything else while enjoying it. If the television is off, no one is talking to you, you aren't reading the newspaper, you are simply experiencing your treat, then that tiny bit will be plenty. You'll feel supremely satisfied. And so elegant, too!

*Chapter 6*

# Meditation for Peace of Mind

Meditation is one of the most widely practiced stress management techniques worldwide. Meditation is an excellent way to cultivate control over your own mental processes, but in many cultures (including ours), meditation is often practiced for spiritual reasons—stress management is merely a fringe benefit.

## What Meditation Does

Meditation helps to still the constant chatter in our heads so that we can think more clearly. It cuts through all our expectations and attitudes. It cultivates mental discipline and, in addition, is exceptionally relaxing.

Whatever your reason for meditation, the effects are consistent. Meditation has a profound effect on both the body and the mind.

Meditation teaches us, most significantly, to live in the now. Rather than letting our restless minds, worried thoughts, and anxious feelings carry us away into what might happen next or what we could have done before, meditation teaches us to still that mental ruckus. What's left? The perfection of the present moment, in which you are only and exactly what you are, with no need for improvement. And that doesn't leave much room for stress.

## Why Meditation Really Works

Meditation works to relieve stress. Studies show that people who are meditating have lower blood pressure, slower breath and heart rate, and brain waves that signal a state of alert but, at the same time, deep relaxation. Meditation also works to train the mind to avoid negative patterns and thought processes, vicious circles of failure and low self-esteem, even the perception of chronic pain as an intensely negative experience.

The brain is a complex and amazing organ, and meditation can teach you to harness your mind's power, integrate your mind and body, and feed your hungry spirit. Meditation comes in many forms, including sitting meditation, walking meditation, mindfulness meditation, yoga meditation, mantra meditation, mandala meditation, visualization, and even prayer. Whether or not you are affiliated with any specific religious tradition, you can pray, either to God, to Goddess, or toward whatever makes sense for you—the universe, the spirit of love, positive energy. As broad a category as meditation may be, it all boils down to one thing: the honing of focus. Modern life promotes an unfocused mind.

### The Harried Life

We are constantly bombarded with stimuli, from the media, from our environments, from people, from our computers. Television switches shots every few seconds and breaks up each show with commercial after commercial. Movies move fast and don't often demand too much concentration anymore. Work is full of so much to do that it isn't easy or even possible to spend very much time on any one task, even if more time would result in higher quality.

It's a get-it-done-fast-and-move-on-to-the-next-thing-quick kind of life for many of us, and so the mind gets used to multiple points of focus and constantly moving focus. The ability to concentrate becomes irrelevant and, consequently, begins to disappear.

Think of your life as an all-you-can-eat buffet. You've got thirty minutes for lunch, and there you stand with your little plate, faced with a fantastic array of options: three kinds of lettuce, two kinds of tomatoes, carrots, cucumbers, cheese, hard-boiled eggs, hot peppers, olives, broccoli, cauliflower, eight kinds of dressing, cottage cheese, potato salad, macaroni salad, three different marinated salads, a taco bar, a pasta bar, four soups, three breads, ribs, wings, meatloaf, fish sticks, drumsticks, ham, turkey, pork, corn, mashed potatoes, strawberries, cantaloupe, honeydew melon, watermelon, peaches, pears, pineapples, three Jell-O salads, and four different colors of some kind of creamy whipped dessert (are you hungry yet?).

It doesn't take most people long to dive in and start loading their plates with the things they like. You may start out with good intentions—"I'll just get a small salad and a little of one entrée—" but with so many tempting options, most people end up taking just a little of this, and that, and this, and that, and this . . .

What often results is a plate filled with so many different things that it's hard to focus on or fully enjoy any one thing on your plate. It's such an overwhelming variety mounded on that little plate that the pleasure comes in the feeling of indulgent excess, the "Look at all this food!" response.

Never mind the food's quality. That's why all-you-can-eat buffets can get away with food of lesser quality than a restaurant that serves just a little of a few choice dishes. If you're impressed with the array of choices, you won't notice so much that everything isn't exquisite in taste. You might be charmed by the price. "Well, as long as it's all I can eat . . ." Or, maybe you are seduced by the possibilities of sampling lots of things you don't normally get to eat. "Wow. Five kinds of potato salad? I'll have to try them all!" The experience of the all-you-can-eat buffet can even become addictive. You lose sight of the pleasure of the food itself because you have become so enamored with the massive quantities and the impressive arrangement.

Now, let's carry over the metaphor. Life is full of stuff to think about. What you have to do today, what you didn't finish from yesterday, what to wear, where to go, who to go with, how to do things, not to mention what to eat. We've got schedules, lists, assignments, deadlines, and responsibilities. We've got dependents, friends, and pets. We've got houses or apartments and cars or trucks to maintain. Some of us have more than one house, more than one car or truck, even a boat. We've got to worry about looking right, acting right, making a good impression. What do others think of you? How well did you complete that task? How much money do you have and what should you spend it on? Or, should you save it?

The list of things the average human thinks about in one day far exceeds the list of items on any all-you-can-eat buffet, so just imagine how much more deluded and seduced into accepting the unacceptable our minds (like our buffet-abused palates) become.

In everyday life, our minds are pulled in different directions, at a pace that can be described, pretty accurately, as frantic.

When the amount of information coming in and the thoughts being generated from within become overwhelming, we start to forget things, lose things, fail to pay attention, make more mistakes, have more accidents, feel more frustrated and less in control of our lives than ever.

## *Trying to Slow Down*

But it's hard to stop. Thinking and taking in information can be even more addictive than the indulgent prospect of five kinds of potato salad. Have you ever turned the television on to watch while working on your laptop, even though you have a lot to get accomplished and know the din will slow you down and distract you? Have you blasted the stereo while reading or called one person after another on your cell phone while driving the car? We can't stop generating input! We feel comforted, dulled perhaps, or at least lulled by the incessant din of media, noise, distraction.

But the price is high. Going through life without ever really paying attention means going through life as a watered-down, lukewarm version of yourself. Maybe spending your days distracted and only partially aware feels safe because you don't have to confront the big questions, the strong emotions. Or, maybe you would like to cut down on all that distraction but don't have the first idea how to start or, for that matter, time to figure it out.

Going through life with your mind going in so many directions all at once isn't really living, and it certainly isn't living up to your potential.

Meditation puts a slow, painless end to this life-numbing process. It hangs a "closed" sign on the buffet restaurant's door for just a few minutes each day. And those few minutes give your mind the opportunity to slow down, wake up, come out of its stupor, and pay attention. To what? To you. To who you are, how you feel, what you are right now, regardless of all the incoming information, regardless of all the internal worries, anxieties, thoughts, and emotions. Meditation also helps you to pay attention to the world around you while helping you to remain unengaged and caught up in that world. You can step back and look, an uninvolved observer, and that can be pretty enlightening.

## How to Start

If you are interested in starting a meditation practice of your own, first read the following chapter, in which many different meditation techniques are described, to find one that appeals to you. Then, set aside a time each day—first thing in the morning, just before dinner, or just before bed are all popular choices—and practice. Practice, practice, practice.

Learning simply to be is a crucial and significant step toward a lifetime of successful stress management.

At first, meditation can be tough. You'll probably find it hard to keep your mind focused. Soon, you'll learn to recognize your mind's wanderings as natural, and, as you gently redirect your mind to its point of focus, you'll stop judging yourself and learn simply to be.

## Tips for Sticking with It

Once you've started to meditate, you may find that the charm wears off after a few sessions. How do you stick with it so that you can reap all the benefits of a regular, long-term meditation practice?

Here are some tips:

- Stick with one kind of meditation most of the time so that you feel focused and practiced at your chosen technique.
- If you absolutely can't stand the thought of meditating on a given day, choose a different type of meditation, just for a change of pace.
- Put meditation into your schedule just like any other appointment. It's an appointment with yourself, and you should be the most important person in your life!
- Meditate at the same time or times each day, to get into a rhythm and cement your meditation into your schedule.
- If possible, meditate on an empty stomach, either before a meal or two hours after (one hour after a light meal). Your body will be able to focus more easily if it isn't busy digesting.
- Meditate at a high-energy time of day rather than a low-energy time of day. If you are a morning person, meditate in the morning. If you get going at night, meditate at night. You'll lessen your chances of nodding off, and you'll have better focus and concentration.

- Throughout your day, make a point to remember the feeling of meditation. Recalling the relaxing feeling of meditation can re-invoke that feeling, helping to extend meditation's stress-relieving effects all day long.
- Start meditating with a friend. Whether you meditate together, at the same time and/or in the same place, or maintain your separate meditation practices, you can call each other on those days when you don't feel like meditating and give each other encouragement and motivation.

Above all, just keep practicing. Practice, practice, practice. Practice may not make perfect (because nobody's perfect), but practice is what will eventually make dramatic changes in your life, your health, and your stress management mastery.

# Chapter 7

# Types of Meditation

Stress management techniques
that strengthen and reinforce
the body will also help to
strengthen the mind's ability
to resist the negative effects
of stress. But some techniques
directly deal with the
mind—the thought processes,
emotions, intellect, and,
extending beyond the mind,
the quest for spiritual meaning.
Meditation comes in many
shapes and sizes. Here are a
few popular techniques—one
is sure to be right for you.

## Zazen Meditation

Zazen is the sitting meditation of Zen Buddhism, but many so-called "Zennists" who don't practice Buddhism practice zazen. Zazen can be accurately defined as "just sitting" and is exactly that—just sitting. It doesn't require any religious or philosophical affiliation. All it requires is the ability to apply the seat of the pants to the floor and stay there for a while. Sounds easy, you say? Hardly. For those of us accustomed to accomplishing something at every moment of the day, just sitting is quite a challenge.

But just sitting accomplishes something amazing if it is practiced every single day for an extended period of time. The mind becomes calmer. The muscles stay more relaxed.

**Can just sitting really have such an effect on your body?**

Believe it or not, it really can, and you'll only begin to perceive its power if you try it and stick with it.

Stress fails to get the rise out of your body and your mind that it once did. Suddenly, you hold the reins, not your stress. Suddenly, priorities seem clearer, truths about life, people, and yourself seem more obvious, and things that used to stress you out seem hardly worth consideration anymore.

Just sitting doesn't remove you from the world, however. Choosing not to worry, dwell, and obsess about things means you can concentrate on the real business of living. Just sitting teaches you how to be, right now, in the moment. As your mind opens up, the world opens up, too. All those anxieties suddenly seem like ropes that were tying you down. Just sitting can dissolve the ropes and set you free to really be who you are and live the life you want. That may sound like pretty powerful stuff, especially as a result of just sitting there.

### The Power of Zazen

The power of zazen isn't really so mysterious. Just as exercise trains the body and just as regular, targeted exercise can train the body to do truly amazing things (think about gymnasts, acrobats, Michael Jordan . . .), zazen trains and exercises the mind.

All those worries and anxieties, the panic, the nervousness, the restlessness, the inner noise are holding you back from your true potential the same way being out of shape and undisciplined holds you back from athletic potential. Just sitting is the way to train your mind to let that stuff go.

From the Buddhist perspective, zazen is thought to be the path to enlightenment because thousands of years ago the Buddha attained enlightenment while "just sitting" under a bodhi tree in India. He sat and sat and sat and continued to sit, and legend has it that he proclaimed (I'm paraphrasing), "I'm going to sit here until I perceive ultimate truth, and that's final." Supposedly, it took about one night. Then, he understood the meaning of all existence. This was, of course, after six years of intensive searching for truth.

Enlightenment may or may not be your goal. But whatever the case, learning to sit, cultivate stillness and inner silence, and become fully and totally aware of the present moment makes for powerful stress management.

### How to Practice Zazen

You can learn zazen at a zendo, a place where Zennists or Zen Buddhists gather to meditate together. The rules for meditation will depend on the individual zendo and whether or not the zendo is based in Soto or Rinzai Zen (differences include things like whether you will sit facing the center of the room or the wall).

Or, you can learn zazen on your own. While, ideally, you should be able to practice zazen under any circumstances, you can help yourself along, especially in the initial stages, by practicing zazen in a quiet place where you're not likely to be distracted. Set aside about five minutes your first time out, then gradually work up to fifteen to thirty minutes once or twice each day. Increase your meditation session by about two minutes each week.

To begin zazen, sit cross-legged or on folded legs (sitting on your feet), with a firm pillow under your hips so that you aren't sitting directly on your legs. Make sure you are wearing enough clothes to stay warm, or wrap yourself in a blanket. Sit up straight, feeling a lift from the crown of the head toward the ceiling and an open feeling in your spine. (In other words, don't scrunch over.) Keep your shoulders back, your chest open, and place your tongue on the roof of your mouth. Look down, but don't hang your head. Your focus points should be slightly downward and your eyes relaxed. Now, unfocus your eyes just a little so that you don't really see what's in front of you. This will help you to focus inwardly.

Rest your hands in your lap in either of these two positions: Rest your left hand, palm up, in the open palm of your right hand. Bring your thumbs together so the tips touch just slightly; or make your left hand into a loose fist and rest it inside the open palm of your right hand. Rest your hands against your body about two inches below your navel.

Keep your mouth closed and breathe through your nose. At first, practice concentrating by counting each breath. In your mind, count from one to ten, with each full breath (inhalation and exhalation) constituting one number. Or, simply follow your breath, keeping your awareness focused on the sound and feel of your breath moving in and out of your body. Don't try to control your breath. Just notice it.

Soon, you'll probably notice that you aren't paying attention to your breath, or even counting. Your mind has wandered! Notice it, then bring your attention back to your breath. Keep going for five minutes. Once you get really accomplished at focusing, you won't even have to count. You'll just sit, breathe, and be.

### Challenges of Zazen

Does zazen sound too simple to be true? Zazen is simple, but it isn't easy, for several reasons. Let's be frank:

- It's boring, especially at first.
- It's really hard to sit still.
- It's difficult to "just sit" when you know how much you have to do.
- It's hard to justify the time when you don't see immediate results. (We are so impatient!)
- Your mind will try to talk you out of it. Discipline is hard and your mind will resist the effort.
- At first, you'll think you are hopeless and could never do it.

- It's frustrating when you can't concentrate on anything.
- It's frightening to confront some of the emotions that arise unexpectedly.
- Dropout rate is high. Most people don't keep it up long enough to see the benefits.

But what happens if you don't drop out? What happens if you sit through the boredom, sit despite the other things you think you should be doing, sit out the frustration and the fear, sit until you've learned how to really sit still, physically and mentally? The answer is simple: Clarity, peace, acceptance, satisfaction, and, yes, a whole lot less stress.

## Walking Meditation

In Zen, walking meditation (kinhin) is the counterpart to sitting meditation (zazen), but walking meditation doesn't necessarily have anything to do with Zen. It is what it sounds like: meditation on the move. Walking meditation is different from sitting meditation because you have to be thinking about what you're doing so that you don't wander into traffic or bump into a tree. On the other hand, it isn't really so different, because in sitting meditation, you become acutely aware of your surroundings. They just aren't changing the way they change when you walk.

### Walking Fits All

Walking meditation is excellent as an alternative to sitting meditation. Some people like to sit for most of their meditation session but then spend the last few minutes in walking meditation, and for some, who practice sitting meditation for longer periods of time, walking meditation gets the body moving periodically without breaking the meditative flow.

But for most people reading this book, walking meditation is a great way to enjoy walking and reap the benefits of meditation at the same time. It's also great for people who simply refuse to sit still. Walking meditation can be a good way to ease into the meditation concept without the commitment of sitting (and sitting for even five minutes is a fairly serious commitment for some people). It's an enjoyable form of meditation that can serve as the basis for a meditation practice, or as an occasional alternative to any other form of meditation.

### How to Practice Walking Meditation

To practice walking meditation, first decide where you will walk. You can do walking meditation outside or around the room. You should have a prepared path in mind so that you don't spend time thinking about where to go during the meditation. Know exactly where you are going: around the block, to the end of the path, around the periphery of the living room.

Begin by spending a moment focusing and breathing, to center yourself and prepare for the meditation. Then, taking slow, deliberate steps, walk. As you walk, notice how your breath feels as it comes in and out of your body. Notice how your limbs move, how your feet feel, how your hands and arms hang, the position of your torso, your neck, your head. Don't judge yourself as you walk. Just notice.

Once you feel you've observed yourself well, begin to observe the environment around you as you walk. Don't let it engage you. If something you see sets you off on some long, involved path of thought that has nothing to do with how you feel walking through the place you are walking, then as soon as you catch your mind so wandering (and it will so wander), gently bring your thoughts back to your breathing.

While new to walking meditation, stay with your breath for a good long while. Before you can start noticing and focusing on the rest of your body and your environment, you need to be able to focus on the breath. Otherwise, your mind will be all over the place.

Start with five minutes and add two minutes every week until you're up to fifteen to thirty minutes of daily walking meditation. Or, alternate walking meditation with another form of meditation every other day. Or, once you are up to fifteen to thirty minutes of daily meditation, spend the first or last five to ten minutes of each session in walking meditation.

## Mindfulness Meditation

Mindfulness meditation is different than other meditations because it can be practiced anywhere, anytime, no matter what you are doing. It is simply focusing on total awareness of the present moment. Mindfulness meditation is inherent in many other forms of meditation but can also be practiced while walking, running, playing basketball, driving, studying, writing, reading, or eating. Anything you are doing, you can do with mindfulness. Your entire day can be one long mindfulness meditation—although it's pretty hard to sustain.

Mindfulness meditation has been popularized by both Easterners who have come West, such as Thich Nhat Hanh, the Vietnamese Buddhist monk, and Westerners such as Jon Kabat-Zinn, Ph.D., the founder and director of the Stress Reduction Clinic at the University of Massachusetts Medical Center. It is easy to do for short periods. It is tough to do for an extended time, because our minds resist staying in the present moment. But it is a rewarding mental discipline that teaches us to cherish and relish the miracle of the present moment, no matter how ordinary. It is also supremely relaxing and satisfying.

### How to Practice Mindfulness Meditation

Wherever you are, whatever you are doing, you can practice mindfulness meditation by consciously making the decision to be fully and completely aware of everything around you. Notice the impressions from all your senses—see, hear, feel, smell, taste. When your mind begins to think about something else, gently bring it back to the present moment. Don't judge the impressions of your senses. Just observe. You may be amazed at what you notice about yourself and the world around you.

If practicing mindfulness anywhere sounds overwhelming, you can start out practicing it while doing something very specific, like eating. Pick a single thing to eat—not a fancy dish with lots of ingredients, but a vegetable, a piece of fruit, some simple broth, or a piece of bread. Eat it slowly, slowly, and notice everything about the process. How do you bring the food to your mouth? How do you put it in? How does it feel in your mouth? How does it taste and smell? How does the food look? What spurs you to take another bite? How does your body react to the food?

Practicing mindfulness meditation while eating is a good way to hone your mindfulness skills. It is also a way to help overcome mindless eating, a common problem especially among stressed-out Americans.

## Prayer

Several studies that continue to baffle the mainstream medical establishment suggest that when hospitalized patients were prayed for, even when they didn't know they were being prayed for, they recovered more quickly than those who weren't prayed for. These studies suggest that people can experience stress relief if others pray for them.

Any practice of centered, reverential concentration is a form of at least a cousin of meditation, and they all work to relieve stress. The meditation traditions of all cultures have common themes and techniques. The Eastern mantra meditation in which "Om" is chanted is similar to the Western practice of saying prayers.

Many different traditions have many different modes and types of prayer. Prayer can mean whatever you want it to mean for you.

What is prayer? Prayer is a focused, concentrated communication, statement of intention, or opening of the channel between you and divinity, whatever divinity is for you. A prayer can be a request, thanks, worship, or praise to God. It can be an intention of being thankful directed to the universe. It can be used to invoke divine power or an attempt to experience divine or universal energy directly.

### How to Practice Prayer

To practice prayer, first decide what you want your prayer to be. To whom, to what, or toward whom or what is your prayer addressed? What is the substance of your prayer? Are you praying for healing for yourself or someone else? Are you praying for something you want or need? Are you praying to say thank you for everything you already have? Are you praying to praise, to express your inner joy, to release your inner sadness?

Once you have a specific intention in mind, sit or lie quietly in a place where you are unlikely to be disturbed. Focus your thought on your prayer and say it, out loud or in your mind. Stay focused on your prayer and the energy of your prayer. Imagine where it is going. Let your prayer continue to radiate from your heart toward its intended source. As you open this channel from your heart to the outside, also allow a space for a return message. You may be filled with a warm, joyful feeling. Or, you might receive a message. Or, you might not.

Whatever happens, continue to focus on your prayer as it flows from you and don't judge the results. Just let it happen and let this outpouring of positive energy from your heart fortify and strengthen you. Because, as we all know, the more you give, the more you receive!

*Chapter 8*

# Relaxation: Biofeedback and Hypnosis

These two forms of relaxation can be very helpful for slowing down and taking stock of yourself. When you're focused and calm, you're better able to tackle the stresses of your daily life.

## Biofeedback: Know Thyself

This high-tech relaxation technique, designed to teach the body how to directly and immediately reverse the stress response, puts you in control of the bodily functions once considered to be involuntary. Biofeedback was developed in the 1960s and was popular in the 1970s and 1980s. A biofeedback session involves getting hooked up to equipment that measures certain bodily functions such as your skin temperature, heart rate, breathing rate, and muscle tension. A trained biofeedback counselor then guides the patient through relaxation techniques while the patient watches the machine monitors. When heart rate or breathing rate decreases, for example, you can see it on the monitor. You learn how your body feels when your heart and breathing rate decrease. Eventually, after a number of sessions, you learn to lower your heart rate, breath rate, muscle tension, temperature, and so on, on your own.

To find a certified biofeedback counselor near you, search your city on the Biofeedback Certification Institute's Web site at *www.bcia.org*.

Because biofeedback requires special equipment and a trained counselor, it isn't something you can figure out on your own at home, but once you've learned the technique, your vital functions are in your own hands—or head!

## Hypnosis: Hype or Help?

People tend to have preconceptions about hypnosis: the swinging pendulum, the controlling therapist with the German accent, the hypnotized person running around on a stage clucking like a chicken. While hypnosis has certainly been used (or misused) by those seeking applause, hypnosis and hypnotherapy are legitimate tools that are also used to help people put themselves into more positive mental states. Hypnosis is, in essence, deep relaxation coupled with visualization.

Hypnosis is not some mysterious state in which you are completely at the mercy of the hypnotist. While hypnotized, you retain your awareness, but your body becomes extremely relaxed and disinclined to move, your awareness becomes narrow, your thinking tends to become literal, and you become much more open to suggestion than you would be in a nonhypnotic state. This suggestibility is what makes hypnosis work.

During the course of life, we may often want to change things about ourselves—our habits, our reactions to stressful circumstances, our tendency to worry, our inability to sleep—but just telling ourselves, "stop that!" or "just go to sleep!" doesn't often work. We've got so much to do. We are caught up in patterns. Our minds are uncontrolled and racing. We are tense. All these things keep us from doing what we know we should do, such as quitting smoking or worrying too much.

## What Is Hypnosis?

Hypnosis is a state similar to sleep. The body becomes so profoundly relaxed that it ceases to be a distraction. The mind becomes highly focused and, thus, more able to do what we want it to do. This focus makes the imagery we use to direct our behavior and feelings more real, so real that our bodies respond to it. This is nothing new. When watching a movie or even hearing a story, our bodies often respond as if we were part of the action—we may experience a faster heart rate at an exciting part, a surge of emotion at a poignant part, feelings of anger at an injustice.

> Hypnosis uses the body's ability to react to the mind by directing the mind in specific ways while the body is relaxed. That's all there is to it.

## Hypnotherapy

Hypnotherapy is the use of hypnosis by a trained therapist to help the patient heal from the trauma of a past event, reframe negative health habits, or regain control over certain behaviors. Hypnotherapy is frequently used to help people stop smoking or overeating. It is a common therapy for people experiencing chronic fatigue. It is also effective for improving self-esteem, confidence, and social anxiety.

## Self-Hypnosis

You can even hypnotize yourself, although not everyone is as open to being hypnotized. You do have to be willing to try it and to follow the hypnotic suggestions. The following exercises, adapted from *The Relaxation & Stress Reduction Workbook*, by Martha Davis, Ph.D., Elizabeth Robbins-Eshelman, M.S.W., and Matthew McKay, Ph.D. (New Harbinger, 2000), can be used to begin training your mind to respond to suggestion. You can also use these tests to see whether you would be a good candidate for hypnosis. If you don't respond to them after several tries, hypnosis may not be helpful to you.

Just remember—the more open-minded you are, the more likely it is that self-hypnosis will work. The mind is powerful, and wanting it to work is half the battle. Many researchers believe almost anyone can learn self-hypnosis.

Hypnotizing yourself is done pretty much the same way you would hypnotize somebody else. While trained hypnotherapists and hypnotists may be able to hypnotize you right away, with some practice, you can learn to hypnotize yourself. You'll need to decide very specifically what

### HYPNOSIS EXERCISE 1

1. Stand with your feet about shoulder-width apart, your arms hanging loosely at your sides. Close your eyes and relax.

2. Imagine you are holding a small suitcase in your right hand. Feel the moderate heaviness of the suitcase and the way the suitcase pulls your body to one side.

3. Imagine someone takes the suitcase and hands you a medium-sized suitcase. This suitcase is heavier and bulkier than the small suitcase. Feel the handle in your hand. Feel the heaviness of the suitcase weighing down your right side.

4. Imagine someone takes the suitcase and hands you a large suitcase. This suitcase is incredibly heavy, so heavy you can hardly hold on to it, so heavy it pulls your entire body to the right as the weight of the suitcase sinks toward the floor.

5. Keep feeling the weight of this heavy suitcase for two to three minutes.

6. Open your eyes. Are you standing perfectly straight, or has your posture swayed, even a little bit, to the right?

### *HYPNOSIS EXERCISE 2*

1. Stand with your feet about shoulder-width apart, your arms hanging loosely at your sides. Close your eyes and relax.

2. Imagine you are standing outside on a small hill in the middle of an expansive prairie. The breeze is blowing and the sun is shining. It is a beautiful, clear day.

3. Suddenly, the breeze begins to pick up, and the wind starts to blow. You are facing into the wind, and as it blows harder and harder, gusting around you, you feel it pushing you back, blowing your hair back, even blowing your arms back a little.

4. The wind is now so strong you can barely stand up. If you don't lean into the wind, you'll be knocked backward! You've never felt wind this strong, and each forceful gust nearly pushes you off your feet!

5. Feel the strength of the wind for two to three minutes.

6. Open your eyes. Are you standing perfectly straight, or leaning into the wind, even just a little?

## HYPNOSIS EXERCISE 3

1. Stand with feet about shoulder-width apart, both arms straight out in front of you, parallel to the ground. Close your eyes.

2. Imagine someone has tied a heavy weight to your right arm. Your arm has to strain to hold up the weight that hangs from it. Feel the weight. Imagine how it looks hanging from your arm.

3. Imagine someone ties another heavy weight on your right arm. The two weights pull your arm down and down. They are so heavy that your muscles have to tense and strain to hold them up.

4. Imagine someone ties a third heavy weight on your arm. The three weights are so heavy that you can barely keep your arm raised. Feel how the weights pull down your arm.

5. Now, imagine that someone ties a huge helium balloon to your left arm. Feel the balloon pulling your left arm higher and higher, tugging it skyward.

6. Feel the weights on your right arm and the balloon on your left arm for two to three minutes.

7. Open your eyes. Are your arms still even, or is your right arm lowered and your left arm raised, even just a little?

you want to work on, say, quitting smoking or not falling apart every time your mother-in-law comes to visit.

Then, self-hypnosis involves a detailed process of breathing, muscle relaxation, and visualization, beginning with the descent down a staircase to the backward-count of ten to one. After some detailed visualization to engage and focus the mind, the hypnosis session ends with a posthypnotic suggestion to trigger you to act the way you want to act. Phrase the suggestion positively: "I feel strong, confident, and in control of the situation when my mother-in-law is in my house," not, "I don't want to burst into tears every time my mother-in-law makes a comment about my housekeeping ability."

If you're not comfortable doing it on your own, your physician may be able to refer you to a psychotherapist or colleague who practices hypnotherapy or knows someone who does. You might also check the phone book.

After the posthypnotic suggestion, you can bring yourself slowly out of the hypnotic state by counting to ten, telling yourself that at the number ten, you will be alert, refreshed, and wide awake.

# Chapter 9

# More Stress Management Tools

We've already covered a number of highly effective stress management techniques, but many more tools for mastering stress management exist. Browse through this list with a spirit of exciting possibility, in search of stress management tools you can use. Maybe one or more of these will be just what you are looking for.

## Attitude Adjustment

Remember that country song about giving people an attitude adjustment on the top of the head? The attitude adjustment technique in this book has nothing to do with violence. It's about subtly changing your attitude.

Negativity is a huge drain on your energy and exacerbates any stress in your life, magnifying it until it seems huge and uncontrollable. Many people are in the negativity habit. Are you?

What's your attitude? Are you a glass half-full or a glass half-empty type? Do you see the upside or the downside first?

> Being negative is a habit. It may be a habit brought on by lots of past suffering, and that's perfectly understandable.

You can stop being negative right now. Even in suffering, you don't have to be negative. Some people remain positive through tragedy; others despair. What's the difference? Attitude.

How do you change your negative attitude? First, become aware of when you tend to be negative. Keep a negativity journal. Whenever you feel like being negative, don't express it out loud. Write it down in your journal. Once you get it out of your system on the page, you can look it over more objectively later. Eventually (as with any kind of journaling), you'll start to see patterns.

Once you know what kinds of things trigger your negativity (it may be triggered by many things), you can begin to catch yourself in the act. When something unexpected happens, do the first words out of your mouth tend to be a frantic "Oh NO!"? If so, stop yourself after that first "Oh . . ." Notice what you are doing. Tell yourself, "I don't have to respond this way. I should wait and see if a full-blown, all-out 'Oh NO' is really warranted." This stopping of your thought process and your negative reaction can help you be more objective and, eventually, more positive about any situation. Even if, after stopping, you realize that an "Oh NO" really is warranted, you won't be calling wolf at every little mishap. You'll save your "Oh NOs" for when you really need them.

Just like any habit, the more you get used to halting your negative reactions and replacing them with neutral or positive reactions, the less you'll find yourself reacting negatively. Instead of "Oh NO," react with silence, taking a wait-and-see attitude. Or, react with an affirmation: "Oh . . . I can learn something positive from this!"

You might encounter obstacles along the way, and that's to be expected. Maybe in your negativity journal you'll discover that you are comforted by or even enjoy being negative.

It is possible that being negative makes you feel safe: If you always expect the worst, you'll never be disappointed. But obstacles are meant to be overcome. Even if a negative attitude is comforting in some ways, is it worth the drain on your energy and happiness? Keep working through it and being honest with yourself. You may discover that your negative reactions are all about protection and that you can find much better ways to protect yourself than that. How about quality friends, a really fulfilling hobby, a regular meditation practice?

If you are serious about kicking your negativity habit, you can adjust your attitude. It just takes some attention. A method of therapy closely related to attitude adjustment is Optimism Therapy.

### *Optimism Therapy*

So, you think you are a confirmed pessimist? Optimism therapy is like an attitude adjustment but focused on reframing responses as an optimist. Optimism may have a reputation as a deluded view of the world through rose-colored glasses, but, actually, optimists are happier and healthier because they tend to assume they have control over their lives, while pessimists tend to feel that life controls them.

Psychologists determine optimistic and pessimistic character based on a person's explanatory style when describing an unfortunate event. The explanatory style has three parts:

1. **The internal/external explanation.** Optimists tend to believe that external factors cause misfortune, while pessimists tend to blame themselves (the internal factor).
2. **The stable/unstable explanation.** Optimists tend to see misfortune as unstable or temporary, while pessimists tend to see misfortune as stable or permanent.
3. **The global/specific explanation.** Optimists tend to see problems as specific to a situation, while

pessimists tend to see problems as global—
that is, unavoidable and pervasive.

How does an optimist body differ from a
pessimist body? Profoundly. Studies show that
optimists enjoy better general health, a stronger
immune system, faster surgical recovery, and
longer life than pessimists.

Because of their tendencies, pessimists may
feel like they are under more stress than optimists,
even though both are under the same amount of
stress. How the stress feels may directly determine how the body reacts, making the stress
response more severe in pessimists. Optimists are
also more likely to engage in positive behaviors
such as exercising and eating well. Pessimists may
adopt a fatalistic attitude that what they eat or
how much they exercise doesn't matter anyway,
so they might as well do what is easiest.

Pessimists sometimes tend to be more socially
isolated, lonely, or have friends with negative
influences—other pessimists or people with habits that are destructive to health and well-being.

But what if you are a pessimist? Can you change? Sure you can. You just need to engage in a little optimism therapy! Studies show that smiling, even when you aren't happy, can make you feel happy, but optimism extends far beyond a forced smile. Pretending to be an optimist can actually make you feel like one and can help your body learn to respond like an optimist, too.

If your pessimism is temporary or recent, you can probably help yourself through your own personal optimism therapy sessions. At the beginning of each day, before you get out of bed, before you have time to get too pessimistic, say one of these affirmations out loud several times:

- "No matter what happens today, I won't judge myself."
- "My life will improve from the inside out."
- "Today I will enjoy myself in healthy ways."
- "No matter what happens around me, this will be a good day."
- "This can be a good day, or this can be a bad day. I choose to make it a good day."

Then, choose one single area or part of your day and vow to be an optimist in that area only. Maybe you'll choose lunchtime, or the staff meeting, or the time with your kids before dinner. During that period, every time you begin to think or say something pessimistically, immediately replace the words or thought with something optimistic. Instead of responding to a spilled coffee cup with, "I'm so clumsy!" respond with, "Whoops! That cup slipped right out of my hand." Instead of responding to a critique of your work with the thought, "My supervisor always hates my work," change your thought and tell yourself, "She didn't like this part of this particular assignment, but the rest of it was great!" You may feel forced and unnatural doing this at first, but like anything else, the more you do it, the more it becomes a habit.

You can adopt the optimist habit. It's good for your health!

If you are a serious and fully committed pessimist, and/or if you suffer from depression, you could probably benefit from visiting a trained psychotherapist for cognitive therapy. Cognitive therapy is a kind of therapy in which the therapist helps patients discover the effect of pessimistic or depressed thoughts on mood, and also helps patients to discover the ingrained nature of these thoughts in order to catch themselves in the pessimistic act. Cognitive therapy can be very successful for depression, and some studies show it is as effective as antidepressant medication (for many people with depression, a combination of cognitive therapy and medication work best).

## Creativity Therapy

Creativity therapy is the use of drawing, painting, writing, sculpting, or playing music as a form of stress relief and also as a way of dealing with emotional or psychological problems. Art therapy has a long history of helping patients work through problems and unblock creativity through certain techniques, and requires a trained art therapist. Creativity therapy is a more general term for using creativity on your own to help relieve your own stress. Art therapy is a kind of creativity therapy, but it is not the only kind. In creativity therapy, you can write poetry, play the piano, even mold homemade playdough to help relieve your own stress and express your creativity.

Creativity therapy is an excellent way to relieve stress. When you become immersed in creation, you can achieve a kind of intense, all-consuming focus similar to the intense focus and concentration you can achieve through a meditation practice. Allowing yourself to become one with your creation—your painting, your drawing, your poem, your short story, your journal entry, your sculpture, your music—helps you to let go, even for a little while, of the stresses in your life. Your body responds by relaxing, counteracting the effects of too much stress.

As with meditation, creativity therapy teaches your mind to concentrate for a long period of time on a single thing—it's great practice and a great way to hone your mental power.

Creativity therapy can also help you to feel good about who you are. Rather than spending your entire day doing what you're supposed to do or what other people want you to do, creativity therapy gives you a space solely for yourself, during which you can express your innermost thoughts, feelings, problems, anxieties, joys, and the imagery that sits deep within your subconscious waiting to be released.

How do you do it? Set aside thirty to sixty minutes each day. Choose your creative outlet. Maybe you will write in your journal or practice the cello or paint with watercolors or draw the flowers in your garden or dance to classical music in your living room. Whatever you choose, commit to this time as you would to a meditation time. Make it an unbreakable appointment. Then, sit down in a quiet place where you are unlikely to be disturbed, and start creating (or dancing or playing or whatever you are doing).

Try not to look at your creations or analyze your own performance, at least not carefully, until you've practiced creative therapy for one month. When the month is over, look carefully at what you've accomplished. Do you see patterns? Motifs? Themes? Words and images that recur in writing or painting or drawing are your personal themes. Movements or sounds can also have meaning for you, personally, if you are dancing or playing music. Spend some time meditating on what they could mean for you. What is your subconscious trying to tell you?

It doesn't even matter if you don't know how to draw, paint, write poetry, or whatever you choose to do. This is not work to be judged, analyzed, or displayed. This is work that comes directly from your subconscious. It is a process of releasing what you are holding onto, mentally, deep inside. And that feels good.

Here are some tips to remember when engaged in your creativity therapy:

- **As you work, don't stop.** Write or draw continuously. If you stop, you'll be more likely to judge your work.
- **Don't judge your work!**
- **Try creating when you are very tired.** Sometimes fatigue dulls your conscious, organized, critical mind, allowing more images from the subconscious to flow through.
- **Promise yourself you won't read what you wrote or survey what you drew until the session is over.** Otherwise, you're likely to start judging.
- **Don't be critical or disappointed in what you come up with.** There is no wrong way to do this, unless you are judging yourself.

- Stuck? Faced with a blank page? **Just start writing or drawing without any thought or plan,** even if you end up writing "I don't know what to write" for three pages or drawing a page full of stick figures. Eventually, you'll get tired of that and something else will come out.

- **Commit to the process.** Even if it seems like it isn't working at first, thirty minutes (or just ten to fifteen minutes when you first try it) each and every day will yield dramatic results if you stick with it.

- **Don't think you can't do creative therapy because you "aren't creative."** Nonsense. Everyone is creative. Some people just haven't developed their creativity as much as others, and creativity therapy is just as helpful (if not more helpful) for nonartists, who aren't already indoctrinated into how they are "supposed to" create something.

- **Most importantly, enjoy the process!** Creativity therapy is illuminating, interesting, and fun!

## Friend Therapy

Friend therapy is simple: Let your friends help you manage your stress! Research shows that people without social networks and friends often feel lonely, but often won't admit it. Loneliness is stressful. Holding in your feelings is even more stressful.

Some people tend to turn to friends automatically when things get tough. Others tend to isolate themselves during stressful times, just when they could most use a listening ear and a few words of encouragement.

Some people already have a group of friends they can turn to, but when things get stressful, it's often easy to stop calling them. Do you stop returning e-mails, calling your buddies, or going out with your group when you are feeling stressed? Engage in some friend therapy and give those buddies a call. Warn them you are feeling stressed. Ask them to listen without offering advice, if you don't want advice. Or, maybe you do!

If you don't have a ready-to-go group of friends or have lost touch with yours, you may have to start from scratch. One of the easiest ways to make friends is to join something. Take a class, join a club, attend a church, find a support group. You might need to try a few different things before you meet people you can really relate to, but if you keep trying, you'll do it.

Don't use the excuse that you can't fit anything else into your schedule. Set something up with a coworker you like, make an overture to another parent at your child's school during a school event, or call a friend you haven't been in touch with for a while to meet for lunch. You're going to eat lunch anyway, right?

Treating your stress with friend therapy doesn't mean you sit at home alone and wait for your friends to come to you. It means you take the initiative and make contact. Sometimes, it just takes a few words to find someone who is in the same position as you and needs friend therapy, too.

Friend therapy should consist of actual contact with another person—not cyber-contact (although that's better than no contact). Phone contact can be helpful, but nothing beats the real thing. Just being with another person—talking (even if it's not about your problems), having fun, taking a break from the daily routine—is a great way to relax, raise your self-esteem, and have the chance to be there for somebody else, too. You don't have to do anything in particular with your friends to make it friend therapy. You just have to get a social life.

Of course, there are limits to what friends can and should do for you. Part of friend therapy is giving as well as taking. A productive friend therapy relationship should certainly be reciprocal. If you use your friends for constant unloading but never allow them to unload on you, they won't be your friends for long!

*Chapter 10*

# De-Stressing

Stress management techniques are great to add to your routine so that you can manage the stress of daily life. But what about that daily life? What about managing your money, your time, your work, your home—managing your life? There are many ways you can de-stress these daily have-tos by making them simpler, easier, less time-consuming, and even a little more fun.

## Your Money

On the list of things that stress you out the most, how high is money? For many people, money is one of the primary causes of daily stress, usually because we don't think we have enough of it, and sometimes because we have enough but are worried about how we are managing it.

There is a lot more to managing your money than getting the bills paid with a little left over or maintaining a productive portfolio. As humans, we have lived with money in one form or another for thousands of years, and it has become deeply ingrained in our psyches. We have all kinds of hidden and not-so-hidden feelings about money, emotional blocks, obsessions, and pretty strange ideas. The phrase "It's only money" might be something you say sometimes, perhaps to justify an extravagant expense or to make yourself feel better when you don't have any of it, but very few of us really believe that the green stuff is "only" anything.

Money is important to us. It is important to our culture. Some might even say it rules the world. But it shouldn't rule you.

In *The 9 Steps to Financial Freedom*, certified financial planner and investment advisor Suze Orman lists "Seeing How Your Past Holds the Key to Your Financial Future" as step number one. Money memories from childhood can hold the key to how we feel about money right now, even if we don't realize it.

Maybe you grew up knowing a family with a lot of money whose members weren't very kind to you. Did you learn to look askance at people with a lot of money, thinking they surely didn't understand about the important things in life such as love and family? Or, maybe you grew up in a family that didn't have to struggle with money and had contact with a less fortunate family whose members weren't trustworthy. Did you learn to be suspicious of people with low incomes?

Maybe money was highly valued in your family, or not valued much at all. Maybe you were taught to manage it, but many of us weren't given those skills and, as adults, don't have the slightest clue what to do with the money we earn beyond paying the bills and buying the groceries.

Added to our personal experiences are cultural stereotypes galore. Television shows, movies, and books often represent rich people as heartless snobs, poor people as slovenly thieves. Old misers who hoard their riches must be a little crazy. Generous souls who give all their money away must be angelic. Sometimes, it seems like a sin to have or try to get money. Yet, it also seems to be a crime if you don't have enough.

In America, the "middle class" has been consistently held up as the ideal and has grown to be such a broad category that most people now consider themselves to be part of it. Most of us aren't in poverty, but wouldn't call ourselves rich, either. And isn't that what makes us comfortable? Yet, we remain obsessed with money . . . with wealth, with the fear of poverty, with the material objects it can buy. Isn't that what capitalism is all about?

If it's "only money," why does it obsess us so? Money is no simple matter. But that doesn't mean it has to be complicated for you. To de-stress your financial life, you need to do several things:

- Understand exactly how you really feel about money, including your prejudices and pre-conceptions.
- Continue to recognize with vigilance your financial preconceptions so that they don't control you.
- Have very specific financial goals, for both present and future.
- Have a very specific plan to meet your financial goals.
- Know exactly how much is coming in and how much is going out.
- Start by building a financial cushion.

### Have Very Specific Financial Goals

If you don't know exactly what you want your money to do for you, it won't do much for you. No matter how much money you make, whether you dabble in stocks or can't make your monthly rent, you must have specific financial goals. If you know where you are headed, financially, your life will be less stressful. You'll know where you are going, even if it will take a long time to get there.

How much money do you need to be able to spend each month? (Most people underestimate this number.) How much do you want to have saved by retirement? Do you need college funds for the kids? A down payment for a house? Would you like to be able to have extra money for investing? How much do you need in savings to cover your expenses for six months if you should become unable to work?

Make a list of your financial goals, no matter how impossible they seem, either on your own or with the help of a good financial planner.

### Have a Specific Plan

It isn't enough just to have goals. You also have to have a workable plan to meet them. If this seems overwhelming to you, visit a good financial planner to help you. Anybody can work toward financial goals, and financial planners are trained to show you how. Or, if you aren't ready for that or feel you can figure it out on your own, start reading books on the subject.

Part of meeting your financial goals might be focused on how to live on less rather than how to make more. Simplicity, frugal living, and other downscaling trends have been popular in the last decade as people realize they've been making lots of money and not getting much in return in the way of spiritual rewards. Books, Web sites, newsletters, and other sources are rich with information on this trend. Here are some tips for de-stressing your financial life by simplifying your financial needs:

- **Become aware of the way advertising works** and how it tries to make you think you need things you don't really need.
- **Every time you are about to spend money, stop for a moment,** take a deep breath, and ask yourself, "Do I really want this, or do I just think I want this in this moment?"
- **Before you spend money, stop for a moment,** take a deep breath, and ask yourself, "Is this item worth the time out of my life I took to earn the money I'll pay for it?"
- **If you decide you really do want something,** that it really is worth the money for you, even if it would be frivolous to someone else (dinner at a restaurant when you can't face cooking, that one special piece of Early American

pottery you've been seeking for years, that pair of shoes that feels perfect), **buying it will probably be less stressful than letting it go.**

- **Make a list of things you can do with your family and/ or friends that don't cost any money.** Be creative. Then, use that list!

- **Slow down.** You don't have to keep moving, going, spending. Why not relax at home with your family or friends and just do nothing for a change?

- **Drive less.** Walk, bike, or take public transportation more.

- **Do you really need all those extra movie channels?** Would basic cable satisfy you?

- **Cooking can be fun,** and home-cooked meals are less expensive than frozen dinners.

- **How often do you go to your gym?** Are you throwing away money when you'd rather just take a walk or a jog or a bike ride for free? For some people, the gym is really worth it. For others, it's a needless money drain.

- **Growing a garden has an initial investment** (small or large, depending on how frugally you go about it), **but it yields free food** and the opportunity for exercise and fresh air all spring and summer.

- Focus your energy on getting rid of the stuff you don't **need** rather than adding to it.
- Learn the joy and freedom of simple living!

### The Five Golden Rules of No-Stress Money Management

| | |
|---|---|
| #1 | Live within your means. |
| #2 | Conquer your debt. |
| #3 | Simplify your finances. |
| #4 | Know your money. |
| #5 | Plan for the future. |

## Time Keeps On Slippin' . . .

Maybe money doesn't stress you out nearly as much as your basic lack of time. If you never seem to have enough time to get anything finished, you might feel constant, chronic stress. But although technically we all have the same amount of time each day (twenty-four hours), time is mysteriously malleable. Have you ever noticed how an hour can fly by like five minutes or crawl by like three hours? Sometimes, your workday is over in a flash, and sometimes it feels like 5:00 P.M. when it's only 11:00 A.M. Can you make this malleability of time work for you?

Learning how to manage your time efficiently takes some practice, but if you have a plan, time management is easy.

You bet you can! Although they say "time flies when you're having fun," time also flies when you are scattered and disorganized. If you have three hours to get something done and you don't manage your time efficiently, those three hours will fly by in a rush of half-finished jobs and flitting from task to task with dispersed energy.

If, instead, your time is organized and you are able to devote your full concentration to one task at a time, time seems to expand in quantity and quality. You get something—even one thing—finished. You feel a sense of satisfaction. The time won't crawl by, like it does when you are enduring something unpleasant. The time may seem to go fast, but because you will have accomplished something, you'll enjoy a feeling of accomplishment, a boost of self-esteem, and the relief of stress.

There are many great books and even Web sites will help you to get organized and manage your time. Begin managing your time to free yourself of the unnecessary stress that comes from scattered energy and the inefficient use of your day by observing the following Ten Commandments of Time Management.

### 1. Start Small

If you start with too many goals, too long of a to-do list, or too high expectations for yourself, you are setting yourself up for failure. Begin with one single time management step, such as laying out your clothes for the next day the night before, to save time in the morning, or by vowing that the counters will be free of dirty dishes every single night, to ease the breakfast rush. As you master each step, you can add more.

### 2. Identify Your Time Management Issues

Are you perfectly efficient at work but your time management skills fall apart in the unstructured, unscheduled environment of your home? Are you able to keep the house straight but whenever the family is home, life seems rushed and hectic, with no relaxed "together time"? Do you spend all day dealing with other people's crises and taking care of busywork, never getting enough time to sit down and really concentrate on your job? Know your trouble spots—the places where time is getting frittered away.

### 3. Identify Your Time Management Priorities

Make a list ranking the things on which you most want to spend your time. Would you like to add family time first, then household organization time, then some personal time? Would you like more time for work and less time for dealing with other people's crises? Would you like to make time for your favorite hobby, time for yourself, or time for romance? Would you just like more time to sleep?

### 4. Focus on Your Top Five

Look at the top five items on your Time Management Priorities list. Focus on those. Be very wary of letting yourself take on anything that takes your time if it isn't focused on one of your top five priorities.

### 5. Have a Strategy

When the day starts, know where you are going. Know what you will do. Time unplanned is often time wasted. That doesn't mean you can't allow for spontaneity or a lovely, unplanned, unscheduled hour or two. Even a whole day of purposefully unplanned time is well worth it. But time unplanned in which you frantically try to accomplish ten different things is time wasted, and that's stressful. Resources abound for helping you make a strategy that works for you.

### 6. Just Say No

Your time is valuable, even more valuable than money. Why should you just give it away to anyone and anything that asks for it? Learn to say no to requests for your time unless that time spent would be something very important to you. You don't have to be on the committee. You don't have to join that club. You don't have to go to that meeting. Just say no and watch that stress that was waiting to descend upon your life float away in another direction.

### 7. Let It Go

If you've already taken on too much, learn to start purging. Don't let anything waste your time. Time spent relaxing by yourself isn't wasted if it refreshes and rejuvenates you. Time spent pacing and worrying is wasted time. Time spent enduring a committee meeting you don't really enjoy is wasted time. Time spent actively engaged in a committee whose cause inspires you is time well spent. Cut out the dross and let everything go that isn't really important.

### 8. Charge More

If you are self-employed, don't waste time on jobs that don't pay you for what your time is worth. (This is difficult until you are well established.) But this rule doesn't just apply to work and actual money. Everything you do takes time. Is the reward payment enough for the time spent? If it isn't, ditch it.

### 9. Do It Later

Do you really need to do every single cleaning chore every day? Do you really need to check your e-mail every ten minutes? Do you really need to change the sheets, vacuum the car, mow the lawn today? If doing it later is just procrastination, you'll spend the saved time worrying. But sometimes, when your time is at a premium, you can relieve your stress and make your life easier by postponing the less crucial chores. Even though many chores do need to be accomplished, they don't always need to be accomplished right now.

### 10. Control Your Time

Remember that not having enough time is always an excuse, never a reason. You can make time for anything if it's important enough. You just have to stop spending time on something less important. You have control over your time. Time doesn't control you.

## Stress-Proofing Your Work Life

For a few lucky people, jobs are sources of rejuvenation, personal satisfaction, and stress relief. For many others, even though work is sometimes or often rewarding, it is also a major source of stress. The more people work and the longer the workday becomes, the more we dream of being able to retire early. Who doesn't waste just a little time thinking about what we would do if we won millions in the lottery? Would we finally tell off our bosses? Quit with a flourish? Never work again?

Actually, research that has followed up on the life satisfaction of lottery winners reveals that very few were happier and that many were less happy after quitting their jobs (winning the lottery brings about its own kind of stress). Although any job can be stressful and sometimes monotonous, our work lives often bring us more than a paycheck. We gain self-esteem, purpose, and a sense of worth from our jobs. We benefit from the social contact, the structure, and the responsibility.

But maybe your job isn't giving you these benefits. Perhaps you should consider a change. Nowadays, people are more likely to change careers more often than ever before, voluntarily or not. Is a job change in order for you? Examine the following list. How many items apply to you?

✓ I dread going to work on most days.
✓ I come home from work too exhausted to do anything but watch television or go to bed.
✓ I am not treated with respect at my job.
✓ I'm not paid what I'm worth.
✓ I'm embarrassed to tell people what I do for a living.
✓ I don't feel good about my job.
✓ My job doesn't allow me to fulfill my potential.
✓ My job is far from being my dream job.

✓ I would quit in a second if I could afford it.

✓ My job is keeping me from enjoying my life.

If two or more items on this list apply to you, you might want to consider a job change. If you aren't qualified to do what you want to do, you need a plan. Find out what would be involved in getting trained in a field that holds more interest for you. Work on saving up some money so that you can start your own business. If you aren't sure what you would like, visit a career counselor who can help you discover what kind of work might be more fulfilling for you.

If you like your job but certain aspects of your work are more stressful than you can comfortably handle, you can take steps to get your job stress under control. Remember, some stress can be good. It can get you motivated and boost your performance. You just don't want to exceed your stress tolerance level—at least not too often.

First, identify what areas of your work life are causing you the most stress. Maybe the work itself is fine but the coworkers are difficult. Or, maybe it's the other way around. Of course, how you manage the stressors at your job depends on what those stressors are. You can take a few different approaches:

- Avoid the stressor (such as a stressful coworker).
- Eliminate the stressor (delegate or share a hated chore).
- Confront the stressor (talk to your supervisor if he or she is doing something that makes your job more difficult).
- Manage the stressor (add something enjoyable to the task, give yourself a reward after completion).
- Balance the stressor (put up with the stress but practice stress-relieving techniques to balance out the effects).

Work is a big part of your life. If you can do something to avoid, eliminate, confront, manage, or balance the stress that comes from your work life, your entire life will be more balanced and less stressful. The key is to deal with the stressor in some way rather than ignoring it and letting the negative effects from work stress build until you are so stressed that you begin to miss work or find yourself putting your job in jeopardy.

## Stress Management Forever

You've got the tools. You've got the knowledge. But the days go by, and, somehow, there never seems time to do anything about it. Can't you start your stress management tomorrow . . . later . . . when you have time?

No, because you won't ever have time. Tomorrow will become today, later will become yesterday, and you'll still be just as busy as you are today. If you don't start to de-stress now, it may never happen.

Maybe you can't join a gym today. But can you take a walk? Maybe you can't overhaul your junk-food diet today, but can you order the chicken Caesar salad instead of the double bacon cheeseburger? Maybe you aren't up for meditation tonight, but can you go to bed a little bit earlier?

Any major life change starts with little steps. You can weave stress management into your life one thread at a time. Luckily, you can work a daily antistress regimen into your routine with very little effort while enjoying a big payoff. Anything you do to help relax your body and calm your spirit is a positive step. To start establishing your new habits today, try doing just four little things every day. Only four, and they don't have to take very long. You can work them into your schedule in any way that works for you. You may already be doing some or all of them.

1. Do something good for your body.
2. Do something to calm your mind.
3. Do something to feed your spirit.
4. Do something to simplify your environment.

Doing one thing to maintain your sense of well-being in each of these categories each day is all it takes to begin a lifelong habit of stress management. What will you do? Any of the techniques listed in this book can be used to fit into these categories. You can even knock off two categories in one blow: Meditate for mental and spiritual maintenance. Then, add a brisk walk for physical maintenance and get rid of one stack of clutter you don't use or need.

Or, maybe you'll choose the body scan in the morning, yoga in the afternoon, twenty minutes of undisturbed quiet time listening to music in the evening, and dropping one of the activities in your life that you no longer enjoy.

Still too complicated? Eat a salad (body), turn off the television (mind), tell a friend how much you appreciate her (spirit), and throw away one thing you've been keeping around for no good reason (simplify).

You probably already have some ideas of how you can work these four antistress steps into your day. Don't feel like you have to keep them the same each day, either. Part of the fun is changing them from time to time, if you thrive on change. If you love your rituals, doing the same things each day is fine, too.

There are other ways to keep your body, mind, and spirit well fed that take only minutes. You can work in exercise time, meditation time, and time for any of the other techniques listed previously in this book. In addition, in the following sections, we'll look at some quick, easy, and practically effortless ways to boost your daily antistress regimen to new heights of effectiveness. You'll feel special implementing these small changes . . . and you are!

# Chapter 11

# De-Stressing for Women Only

Stress comes in many shapes and sizes, and it also comes in different ways, depending on who you are. Women have unique and particular symptoms of and reactions to stress because of their biology and because of culture. The aging process is stressful for biological, psychological, and cultural reasons, making stress for seniors another unique experience.

## A Woman's World of Stress

It has been only in recent years that research organizations have begun to pay more intention to health issues in women, but women have known all along that being a woman can be stressful—biologically speaking and, certainly, culturally speaking as well.

Most of us have an easier time, physically, than our grandmothers and great grandmothers. For our grandmothers, taking care of a home, cleaning, cooking food, and washing clothes were incredibly labor-intensive. Of course, now, we've got automation to help us with many of the household chores. In addition, it has become socially acceptable as well as expected that men will help out at home. So, what are we stressed about?

Women may not have to do the laundry by hand anymore, but we've got plenty of other things to take up that saved time. We've got jobs, often impossibly demanding jobs. We've got financial pressure, relationship pressure, pressure to look good no matter what our age, pressure to be in shape, in charge, in control— pressure to be all that women have always been and more. Many of us are also juggling houses, spouses, and children. If we've left off any of the "requisite" parts—if we aren't married, didn't have children, decided not to work outside the home—we are bombarded with criticism. Sometimes, the criticism comes from within, in the form of worry, anxiety, panic, guilt, and fear. If the world doesn't expect us to do it all, we expect it of ourselves.

On top of everything else, women go through several intense hormonal changes during their lives and hormonal fluctuations each month. These hormonal fluctuations can compound the feeling of stress, and stress can, conversely, affect a woman's hormonal levels. So, what's a stressed-out woman to do? First, let's look at what we're dealing with.

## Female Stress Mismanagement Syndrome

Studies show that, when under stress, women are more likely than men to communicate with others and talk through their concerns. This is a healthy reaction to stress and a tendency women should be proud of. However, the reliance on others to be a source of advice and opinion can easily turn into something that actually becomes a source of additional stress.

Even in the twenty-first century, women tend (there are, of course, many exceptions) to be more concerned with how others perceive them than men are. Little girls are still encouraged (not necessarily by their parents but by others, including the television) to be passive, pleasing to others, helpful, polite, and a team player, and to learn the rules of socially acceptable behavior.

While little boys are also taught these things, in general, society as a whole tends to be more accepting of and make more excuses for boys who bend the rules a little or who aren't always quiet and polite. "Oh, boys will be boys. What are you going to do!" people are likely to imply with knowing smiles. Boys tend to get the message that independence, spirit, competitiveness, and even aggression are appropriate. Girls are rewarded for docility and social correctness.

Because women learn at such an early age that how they look and how helpful and agreeable they are impact how they will be judged, women sometimes overemphasize appearance and socially acceptable behavior, perpetuating the stereotypes of which they are the victims. Society continues to reward us for doing so. The price is an unreasonable level of stress if we are seen looking bad; do something rude; work at a job that has traditionally been dominated by men; keep a messy house; attempt to supervise unruly children; are an assertive and take-charge boss, manager, or CEO of a company; or (believe it or not) are professionally successful at all! What will people think? What will people say?

To conquer female stress mismanagement syndrome, you don't have to start undermining your own good habits, but it is a good idea to practice doing things for yourself and the people you care about, rather than focusing on the judgments and opinions of people you hardly know. Whenever you are feeling stressed about what someone else thinks (or what you think someone else thinks), ask yourself these questions:

- Am I really bothered by what someone else thinks, or am I bothered because secretly I agree with them? (If this is true, reframe your worries from your own point of view.)
- Am I stressed about what others think out of habit? Do I really care?

- What is the worst thing that could happen if somebody doesn't approve of me?
- What do I really think is important in this situation, regardless of anybody else's opinion?

It's nice to know how to be polite and how to help others. It's nice to know how to keep your house neat and cook a satisfying dinner. But it's also nice to achieve career success, be independent and spirited, know how to get what you need in life, and not have to depend on anybody else to take care of you. People who don't see your positive qualities have narrow vision.

## The Estrogen Connection

One of the things that makes a woman a woman is the presence of the female sex organs and the particular hormone cocktail that is heavy on the estrogen and light on the testosterone. Estrogen and related hormones govern an amazing number of bodily functions, from ovulation to skin clarity. By menopause, estrogen levels in a woman's body have dropped by about 80 percent, causing many changes in the body, from hot flashes to osteoporosis.

Estrogen is the reason why women have a lower rate of cardiovascular disease than men. Estrogen has a protective effect on the heart. After menopause, men and women have about the same risk of heart attack, and women are more likely to die from their first heart attack than men.

But during periods of stress, estrogen levels drop temporarily because the adrenal glands are busy pumping out stress hormones instead of estrogen. These estrogen dips cause little windows of menopause-like cardiac vulnerability. Studies have shown that when subjected to stress, estrogen levels drop; during that period, the arteries in the heart immediately begin to build up plaque, leading to a higher risk of heart disease. Stress may actually cause damage to artery walls in addition to plaque buildup. Little nicks and tears from cortisol can speed up the accumulation of plaque on artery walls. Keeping estrogen levels constant by keeping stress in check is just one more reason to manage stress during your childbearing years.

## Which Came First, Stress or PMS?

That time of the month. Our monthly friend. A visit from Aunt Flo. The lady in red. No matter what we call it, menstruation is a potential source of monthly stress for almost half a woman's life. Menstruation is often accompanied by discomfort. PMS, or premenstrual syndrome, can cause additional physical discomforts and emotional symptoms such as irritability, sadness, depression, anger, or exaggerated emotions of any kind.

Serious cases of PMS can be treated medically. If you get just a little emotional, a little bloated, a little achy, or gain a few pounds every month before or during menstruation, the best thing to do is step up your stress management efforts in a few specific ways that emphasize self-care. You might notice that many of these steps are basic stress management strategies you can do at any time to help relieve stress, but if you've been forgetting, this is the time to reinstate your good habits:

- Be sure to drink those eight glasses of water to combat bloating.

- Get plenty of sleep. Go to bed early.
- Avoid caffeine, sugar, and saturated fat.
- Eat plenty of fresh fruits, vegetables, and whole grains. You need the fiber and you'll feel more balanced.
- Drink extra milk and eat more yogurt. Studies show that calcium may be among the most effective treatments for the symptoms of PMS.
- Take it easy. If you really don't feel like staying out late or pushing yourself, don't.
- Relieve cramps by curling up in bed with a heating pad, a cup of herbal tea, and a really good book.
- Soak in a warm bath.
- Take ibuprofen (like in Advil or Motrin), which can help relieve cramps.
- Meditate, focusing on relaxing and warming your abdominal area.
- Get a massage.
- Research woman's history. What a good time to celebrate being a woman!
- One week after your period is over, do a monthly breast exam. Report any suspicious lumps, thickening, or changes to your doctor.

And don't forget that yearly pelvic exam! One of the best ways to stay healthy is to catch health problems early, when they can be treated much more easily.

## Stress and Menopause

Stress doesn't cause menopause. Aging causes menopause, and that's just the way it is. Remember that adage about changing the things you can change, accepting the things you can't change, and having the wisdom to know the difference? This is one of those things you can't change. If you are a woman, eventually you'll go through menopause.

If stress is often about change, then they don't call menopause "the change" for nothing. Menopause can be very stressful to both mind and body. Menopause is marked by plummeting estrogen levels, and the results can be hot flashes, depression, anxiety, a feeling of flatness or loss of emotion, wildly fluctuating emotions, vaginal dryness, loss of interest in sex, loss of bone mass, increased risk of cardiovascular disease and stroke, increased cancer risk . . . and the list goes on.

Could there possibly be a positive side to menopause?

Menopause is more than just a hormonal adjustment. Fortunately, many of the changes associated with menopause are temporary. While your risk of certain diseases will remain higher after menopause, the hot flashes, the depression, the mood fluctuations, even the loss of sex drive are all temporary.

Stress management techniques can help to alleviate or reduce many of the temporary side effects of menopause. Meditation and relaxation techniques coupled with regular moderate exercise including strength training are just the one-two punch your uncomfortable symptoms need. If you seek hormone replacement therapy (it's controversial, so talk to your doctor), you may be able to further alleviate many of the temporary symptoms of menopause, too. This will free you to focus on the good stuff: the new you!

You are still you after menopause, of course, but there is something liberating about moving to the next stage of life, postchildbearing. Even if you never had children, knowing you are past that stage in your life when people will ask you when you are going to have them is a freedom.

You've also moved to a stage in life where you can be the center of your universe again. That doesn't mean that you need to become selfish. You can still devote time to helping family, friends, children, and grandchildren.

For many seniors, however, this isn't so easy. Just when your life was about to become your own again, you find yourself sandwiched: caring for elderly parents and primary baby-sitter to your grandchildren. Chances are increasing that your own adult children are even moving back in. Help! Maybe you love helping your family, but as you enter your post-childbearing stage of life, it is crucial for your own happiness and sense of well-being that you also devote some time to yourself. It isn't selfish. If you are happier, calmer, and more fulfilled, you'll also be more helpful to others in a productive (rather than a codependent) way. Make yourself a top priority, as you continue to love and support your parents and offspring. Don't let your life slip away without fully appreciating what you've accomplished. Keep your eye on the big picture.

## Stress and the Senior Woman

Once you've passed the childbearing years, life begins to open up. You feel more secure, you know who you are, you have time to yourself. But the golden years can be stressful for women. Beloved children move out, and the house seems empty. Bodies get achier and less agile.

If you've worked most of your life and are now retiring, you may find yourself suffering from stress just when you thought you were taking a load off by leaving your job. Jobs are often a great source of self-esteem as well as money. Now, money may be tight after retirement, and the house may seem tight, too, when you and your partner are suddenly at home all day together. Even if you have plenty to do, you may feel like your work is less important because you aren't being paid for it or because you aren't getting direct feedback from a supervisor. You aren't used to being your own supervisor!

If you are far from relatives and friends, life may get lonely. Health problems are stressful, and depression is common in older women. What can a senior woman do to combat the negative effects of stress?

- **Stay engaged.** Participate in activities outside your home, whether volunteering, exercise classes, art classes, language classes, book groups, church, cooking classes, or social groups. You'll stay fired up about what's going on around you, and you'll keep your mind active, which helps to keep you feeling young.
- **Don't lose touch with friends.** Make an effort to stay connected. Maintain a mix of friends your own age—and younger friends, too.
- **Consider getting a pet.** Pets are proven to reduce stress and can provide you with a lasting and satisfying relationship. Small dogs and cats are easy to handle and give back tenfold what you give them. Birds can also be rewarding companions, and you can teach them to talk!
- **Stay active.** Take a walk or do some other kind of exercise every day. Walking alone or with friends is beneficial physically and emotionally.

- **Pay attention to what's going on in the world.** Talk about events with your friends and/or your partner. Work on being open-minded; make sure you can back up your opinions with good reasoning.
- **Try yoga** to help keep your body flexible and less prone to injury.
- **Eat nutrient-dense foods with plenty of calcium, protein, and fiber.** Soy foods may also help with the effects of menopause. Try vanilla or chocolate soymilk.
- **Lift weights** to keep your bones strong and to combat osteoporosis.
- **Keep drinking lots of water** and getting enough sleep.
- **Consider qualified holistic health care practitioners,** who may be inclined to put you on fewer medications and help you to adjust your whole lifestyle for better health.
- **Meditate daily** to explore the universe of the inner you. Get to know yourself all over again!
- **Keep your mind busy.** Take up a new hobby. Learn a new language. Read books in a different genre. Do word puzzles. Have intellectual discussions with your friends.

- **Do things for other people.** Service to others will make you feel good about yourself as well as help other people.
- **Start working on writing your life history.** You'll enjoy sorting through the memories, and your manuscript will be a valuable family treasure.
- **Value yourself.**

*Chapter 12*

# For Men Only

You are stressed, and it's no wonder. Men are expected to do more than ever before—be both provider and nurturer, strong and emotionally available, independent and supportive. Men may feel stress if they aren't always confident and strong, or if they aren't willing to share their emotions.

## Male Stress Mismanagement Syndrome

Studies show that men and women tend to handle their stress differently. Women talk about their problems with others. Men don't. Instead, men tend to seek out the company of others, minus the sharing. Or, men turn to physical activity.

Both methods can work well, but men's stereotypical reluctance to express feelings can lead to increased negative effects of stress, including a sense of isolation, depression, low self-esteem, and substance abuse. Men are four times more likely than women to commit suicide, and men are more likely than women to abuse drugs and alcohol and commit violent acts.

How can you help yourself manage your own stress and combat your tendency to keep it all inside? Here are some tips for better male stress management:

- **Don't feel like talking about it?** Write about it. Keep a journal to vent. Even if you don't feel like writing about how you feel, once you get going, you may find it very therapeutic.
- **Exercise** is an excellent way to release pent-up anxiety, anger, or feelings of depression.

- **Drink more water.** It makes everything work better.
- **Cut down on the caffeine.** Caffeine can make you feel more anxious, and it can raise your blood pressure.
- **Try meditation** or other relaxation techniques.
- **Use humor** to diffuse tense situations.
- If you feel like your feelings are out of control, **talk to a counselor or therapist.** Sometimes it's easier to talk to somebody who isn't part of your personal life.

## Real Men Do Feel Stress

Men are taught to be independent and strong, to deal with things rationally and logically. Sometimes, this approach can be an effective way to handle a crisis, to get things accomplished, or to let things go that aren't worth dwelling on. But sometimes, rationality and strength don't address the real problem, which doesn't go away. Some men turn to drugs, alcohol, or other addictions such as gambling or sex to numb the pain or sadness or anxiety that come from too much stress. Many men get depressed, but far fewer men than women are likely to admit it or seek help for their depression.

Sometimes, not feeling the stress makes it worse. Eventually, the stress will take over and force you to feel it. The best way to ensure you remain in control is to manage the stress as it comes. Let yourself recognize it so that you can deal with it.

Recognize that "manliness" and everything that word implies for you could be interfering with your ability to manage your stress. Life doesn't have to be a competition. Success isn't always measured in dollars and prestige. You don't have to get by on five hours of sleep or try to keep up with your buddies at happy hour after work.

And you don't have to deny that you are feeling stressed. You don't have to tell everybody you meet, but you don't have to deny your stress to yourself. You can manage your stress in many ways that can make your life easier, and you can do many of the techniques that relieve stress alone in your own home. It's your business.

## Testosterone Connection

Studies have linked both physical and psychological stress to a drop in the level of testosterone, the hormone that gives men their masculine qualities such as facial hair growth, musculature, and deep voice. Testosterone is a hormone with a complex relationship to behavior: Testosterone levels can influence behavior, and behavior can influence testosterone levels. In ancient times, when some men were castrated (such as the eunuchs that served royalty in many different countries throughout history, or the Italian castrati with their beautiful, high voices), they would tend to be more docile, have a reduced sex drive, and develop more body fat.

Testosterone has been linked to dominant behavior in men. It is in part responsible for the male perspective and the feeling that control, rationality, and dominance are desirable traits in men. Countless studies that assert the differences between the genders in communication style, learning style, and even basic understanding of language are exploring the relationship between people who are driven more by testosterone and those driven more by estrogen.

Studies have shown that women tend to be attracted to men with more masculine features and more dominant behavior—not aggressive behavior, necessarily, but dominant behavior. While cultural factors certainly modify biological impulses and while there are many exceptions, masculine features and dominant behavior are biological signals of reproductive fitness.

Traditionally, in our culture, men went out to earn a living and support their families, fulfilling this urge to dominate. The estrogen- and oxytocin-driven females stayed at home, accomplishing the nurturing of children and caretaking of the home. But life today seems much more complex than it once was (although surely we oversimplify the past). As our society's needs evolve, its members don't like to be restricted to a certain role. Many women get enormous satisfaction from earning a living outside the home and supporting their families. Many men get immense satisfaction from staying home to raise their children, and they do an excellent job at being caretakers. These so-called reverse roles aren't really reversed at all. Maintaining a household and raising children can fulfill a man's need to accomplish something important. A stay-at-home dad can be a dominant figure in a very positive way for his children. Household maintenance can be a matter of competition and pride.

Women, too, tend to excel in the working world by being communicative, empathetic, and nurturing. In other words, both men and women can do any kind of job, but they will tend to go about it in different ways. You may not run the house or care for the children in the same way as your partner, but that doesn't mean your way isn't just as good.

The point is that a man does not necessarily become frustrated or stressed just because he isn't doing the traditional "man" things. But, in fact, stress sets in when a man isn't allowed to be who he needs to be. The propensity toward dominance can result in feelings of stress when dominant individuals are placed in subordinate positions. If men are forced to act subordinate when it isn't in their nature—even if that means having to be subordinate to a controlling CEO—the result can be lots of stress. If left unchecked, that stress can turn into aggression or other forms of anti-social behavior. If men aren't able to fulfill their need to control their own situation, go out there and compete, and feel like they are making an important contribution, they may feel frustrated and unfulfilled.

What happens when stress depresses a man's testosterone level? A lowered level of testosterone could result in a drop in self-confidence and feelings of control, which can exacerbate an already stressful situation. This can be frustrating and can provoke anxiety in men who are used to feeling dominant. To maintain your health and confidence, it is crucial that you manage your stress. If you keep your testosterone level in balance, you'll feel better, and you'll be more confident and more in control of your feelings and actions. The best way to do this is to keep stress in check.

## Your Stress, Your Reproductive Fitness

Stress can lower testosterone production. And lower testosterone levels result in a lower sperm count, which can drastically reduce a man's reproductive fitness. If you and your partner are trying to get pregnant, stress management is just as important for you as it is for her. How can you get back on the reproductive track? The same way your partner can. Do it together:

- Get daily moderate exercise.
- Eat healthy foods.
- Get sufficient sleep.
- Drink plenty of water.
- Meditate or practice relaxation techniques daily.
- Practice breathing deeply.
- Make a conscious effort to have a positive attitude.
- If you really aren't able to control something, let it go.

## Anger, Depression, and Other Unmentionables

Stress can have some specific effects on men that, although often very treatable, can make men feel lost, frustrated, or hopeless. Anger management is an important skill for men. Your naturally higher testosterone level can make you more prone to anger and aggression than women (there are certainly exceptions). Suppressing anger can be just as dangerous as venting anger inappropriately. Both cause a surge in stress hormones that can be harmful to the body.

Frequent anger can also be a sign of depression. Depression is a very real problem for many men, who tend to be less likely to admit they are depressed or to seek treatment. Here are the signs of depression:

- Feeling out of control
- Excessive irritability or anger
- Loss of interest in things that you previously enjoyed
- Sudden change in appetite (much higher or lower)
- Sudden change in sleep patterns (insomnia or sleeping too much)
- Feelings of hopelessness and despair
- Feelings of being stuck in a situation with no way out
- Anxiety, panic
- Frequent crying
- Thoughts of suicide
- Sabotaging success (such as quitting a good job or ending a good relationship)
- Substance abuse
- Increase in addictive behaviors
- Decreased sex drive

If you are depressed, please seek treatment. Depression is easily treatable, through therapy, medication, or a combination of both. Once you are over the first hurdle, you will feel better about yourself and will be more able to implement lifestyle changes, such as daily exercise, that will help to further alleviate depression.

### *Pressures Everywhere*

Men often feel that asking for help is a sign of weakness, but in the case of depression (and in many other cases, for that matter), asking for help is a sign of strength. The situation is never hopeless! Ask for help.

Another area of concern for many men, and something that can be a direct result of even minor and/or temporary stress, is erectile dysfunction (ED), or impotence. Isolated incidents of being unable to maintain an erection sufficient to complete sexual intercourse are normal. Being overly tired, drinking too much, having a bad day, or putting too much pressure on yourself to perform can all result in an incident. But if the condition persists—if you cannot maintain an erection at least half the time you try—then you could have erectile dysfunction, and erectile dysfunction can be caused by stress.

### Other Causes

There are other causes. In men over fifty, the most common cause of ED is circulatory problems such as hardening of the arteries. It isn't just the arteries in your heart that can harden with age. The arteries to the penis can also get clogged, preventing sufficient blood flow for an erection. ED can also be a symptom of a serious disease such as diabetes, or kidney or liver failure. It can be caused by nerve damage to the area from disease or surgery, including spinal surgery, or surgery on the colon or prostate. ED can be a side effect of many different medications, including antidepressants (very common), medication for high blood pressure, and sedatives. Excessive alcohol consumption can also cause ED, and so can smoking.

But, in many cases, ED has a psychological cause, and, in many cases, that cause is stress. Stress and ED do an insidious dance. You're stressed. You experience an incident of impotence. That makes you more stressed, increasing your chances of it happening again. It happens again. You get more stressed. How do you break the cycle?

In many cases, people who experience ED due to psychological causes will still have erections during sleep or in the morning. It's still a good idea to see a doctor to make sure there isn't an underlying physical condition. If it's clear that the cause is psychological, then you can focus on managing your stress.

See if you can pinpoint the cause. The stress that causes ED can come from any source. Overall life stress can certainly cause it, but other kinds of stress can, too, including the following:

- Stress in the relationship between sexual partners
- Stress caused by fear of poor performance

- Stress caused by a fear of intimacy or a sudden change in the nature of the relationship, such as an engagement
- Fear of disease
- Stress due to unresolved sexual issues including sexual orientation
- Depression and its accompanying loss of interest in sex

If you know or suspect where your stress is rooted, you can begin to work on that area. Practice meditation and relaxation tips. Get enough exercise. If you are afraid of something, talk about it, think about it, write about it, or seek help so that you can work it out and get past it. If you are depressed, seek treatment. If you are having relationship problems, confront them and work them out. Sometimes, all it takes is some open communication.

Or, maybe your ED is a signal that you are having sex with the wrong person. Think about that. Whatever the cause, most psychological causes of ED can be resolved, in which case, your function will return without any sign of having left you. When it comes to ED, "don't worry, be happy" may be easier said than done, but it's still pretty good advice.

## The Midlife Crisis: Myth, Reality, or Stress in Disguise?

While both men and women can experience a midlife crisis, the term is most often applied to men. The midlife crisis may or may not have a hormonal basis, but it is certainly a reality. During this time of life, typically in the late thirties to mid-forties, men begin to question the direction their lives have taken. They wonder if they've missed out on things. They are tired of their jobs, feel their relationships have stagnated, and fear that they have lost interest in life.

What a man does in response to his midlife crisis depends on the man and the intensity of the feelings, but you've all seen the stereotypes on television and in the movies: the divorce, the twenty-something girlfriend, the red sports car. Of course, it doesn't always work out this way. Sometimes, the response is depression, withdrawal, anxiety, or an increasing dissatisfaction with daily life. Sometimes, men change careers at this point in life and go for their dreams.

What does the midlife crisis have to do with stress? Years of chronic stress due to unresolved relationship issues or job dissatisfaction can build up to the final breakdown that is the midlife crisis. Additionally, the midlife crisis becomes a source of stress because of the changes it has effected in life.

What can you do about it? First, before you get to your midlife crisis, learn to manage your stress. This can subvert a midlife crisis; after all, if your life is going just the way you want it to go, you won't have any reason for a crisis. If you're already heading full speed into yours, however, you can help to soften the blow by preparing for the stress-to-come:

- **Make a list of all your unfulfilled dreams.** Look at it and contemplate it. Which of the dreams are unrealistic, things you know you'll never do but just like to dream about? You can cross those off your list for now (or put them on a different list).
- **Look at what's left.** What have you really wanted to do, always intended to do, but haven't yet

accomplished? Think hard about these items. Are they things you really want or things you just think you want? Relax, close your eyes, and visualize having these things. Sometimes we like the idea of something—getting a doctoral degree, having a drop-dead-gorgeous partner, being extremely rich—but when we think about what it would take to get there, we realize it isn't really worth it. Which items do you think probably wouldn't really be worth the effort of getting there? Cross them off the list (or move them to a different list).

- **Why haven't you accomplished these dreams yet?** What would you need to do to make them happen? Start thinking about what you could do to really make these dreams come true. Make a list of steps. If you have a partner, encourage her to make her own list, then talk about how you might both reach your dreams together while you are still young (young is a relative term, after all).

- If your dissatisfaction lies with your relationship, this is the time to do something about it, and that doesn't necessarily mean leaving the relationship behind. **Take steps to revitalize your relationship.** Break up your routine. Take a trip together. Change things around in the bedroom. Be romantic. Put some real attention and focus into your sex life. If you aren't both ready for these changes, discuss the reasons why. If you have past issues to work out, work them out. A professional therapist can be very helpful.

- **Stop doing things you don't like and don't really have to do.** If you really, truly can't stand your job, find a new one or start your own business. More and more opportunities exist for self-employment today, and more and more people prefer to stay close to home and redirect their energies to their homes and to living more in line with their dreams and desires. Can you get by on less money? Then do it. If you cringe at the thought of that committee you are on, that group you joined, or that club you are in, then let it go. Don't waste your life doing things you don't like that aren't necessary.

- **Give to others.** All this self-examination can make you feel selfish. Balance it out with a conscious effort to give your time, energy, or money to people who really need it. You could devote some time to a charity that is meaningful to you or to a cause you believe in, or you could spend more time with your partner, talking to your kids, or playing with your grandchildren.

## Stress and the Senior Man

It isn't easy when your body starts to betray you, and it can be hard to admit that you can't do all the things you could once do. Getting older is stressful for men and sometimes may seem to be fraught with loss: of muscle tone, stamina, sex drive, even hair. Women may say that men get better looking as they age, but men often don't feel better looking as they recognize they have gained weight and lost energy.

Retirement can also add stress in great heaps to your already full plate. The loss of a job, from which you've gained an identity and a sense of worth all these years, can be devastating for men—who suddenly don't know who they are or what to do with themselves. Of course, you aren't your job, and you probably know that, but after fifty years of working, you may feel like you've let go of a big part of yourself.

What can a senior man do to feel strong, confident, and stress-free? Manage that stress, of course! Try some of these tips (they're similar to the tips for senior women listed earlier in this chapter—we're all people!):

- **Stay engaged.** Participate in activities outside your home, whether volunteering, playing on a team, painting classes, writing classes, hobby groups, or church. Take up carpentry or cooking, fly fishing or ballroom dancing. Do whatever interests you. You finally have the time, so don't waste it! Maybe you always wanted to learn the law, or how to speak Italian, or how to be a bird watcher. Staying active will keep you fired up about what's going on around you. It'll also keep your mind active, which helps to keep you feeling young.
- **Don't lose touch with friends.** Make an effort to stay connected. Maintain a mix of friends your own age and younger friends. Plan to do your activities outside the home, along with friends. You might help someone else get out of the house who really needs it!
- **Consider getting a pet.** Pets are proven to reduce stress and can provide you with a lasting and

satisfying relationship. Dogs and cats give back tenfold what you give them. Birds can also be rewarding companions.

- **Stay active.** Take a walk or do some other kind of exercise every day. Walking with friends is beneficial physically and emotionally.
- **Pay attention to what's going on in the world.** Talk about events with your friends and/or your partner. Work on being open-minded but on having opinions you can back up with good reasoning.
- **Try yoga** to help keep your body flexible and less prone to injury. More and more senior men are trying yoga and gaining great benefits.
- **Eat nutrient-dense foods** with plenty of calcium, protein, and fiber.
- **Consider taking a daily zinc supplement** to keep your prostate healthy. Pumpkin seeds are also rich in zinc. The herb saw palmetto may also be good for prostate health.
- **Lift weights** to keep your muscles and bones strong.
- **Keep drinking lots of water** and getting enough sleep.

- **Consider qualified holistic health care practitioners,** who may be inclined to put you on fewer medications and help you to adjust your whole lifestyle for better health.

- **Meditate daily** to explore the universe of the inner you. Get to know yourself all over again!

- **Keep your mind busy.** Take up a new hobby. Learn a new language. Read books in a different genre than you normally do. Work out word puzzles. Have intellectual discussions with your friends. Build stuff.

- **Do things for other people.** Service to others will make you feel good about yourself as well as help other people.

- **Start writing your life history.** You'll enjoy sorting through the memories, and your manuscript will be a valuable family treasure.

- **Value yourself.**

Whether you are a man or a woman, in your twenties or in your nineties, stress can disrupt your health and functioning. But no matter your gender or age, you can do something to lessen the effects of stress in your life. Don't be a victim of your gender or your age. It's your body, your mind, and your life!

*Appendix A*

# Resources

When it comes to stress management, knowledge is power. These resources will help your further your knowledge about stress, good health, good nutrition, and yourself. I've also listed organizations you can contact for more information, therapy, or relaxation and web sites for stress-free Web surfing. Happy explorations!

**Note:** Inclusion of resources in this book does not necessarily imply endorsement of these resources' health-related content, products, or services.

## Books

Benson, Herbert, M.D. *The Relaxation Response*, Updated and Expanded Edition. New York: Avon Books, 2000.

David, Martha, Ph.D., Elizabeth Robbins Eshelman, M.S.W., and Matthew McKay, Ph.D. *The Relaxation & Stress Reduction Workbook, 5th edition.* Oakland, CA: New Harbinger Publications, 2000.

## Organizations and Web Sites

### American Institute of Stress
124 Park Avenue, Yonkers, NY 10703
Phone: 914-963-1200
Fax: 914-965-6267
*www.stress.org*

### National Sleep Foundation
*www.sleepfoundation.org*

### Grief Net online grief support network
*www.griefnet.org*

### Ask Dr. Weil
Andrew Weil, M.D.'s informative Web site on integrative medicine and whole-self health care: *www.drweil.com*

*Appendix B*

# Stress Management

Here is your alphabetical listing of tools, techniques, and therapies for combating the stress in your life.

### applied kinesiology

This is a muscle testing technique that helps people determine where in the body they are experiencing an imbalance or problem. Then, massage as well as movement of certain joints, acupressure, and advice on diet, vitamins, and herbs are offered as treatment.

### art therapy

In art therapy, you can use any art form as an expression of creativity to help release stressful feelings.

### attitude adjustment

Being negative is a habit, and adjusting your attitude to be more positive can be a habit, too. Just like any habit, the more you get used to halting your negative reactions and replacing them with neutral or positive reactions, the less you'll find yourself reacting negatively.

### biofeedback

This high-tech relaxation technique, designed to teach the body how to directly and immediately reverse the stress response, puts you in control of the bodily functions once considered to be involuntary. A biofeedback session involves getting hooked up to equipment that measures certain bodily functions such as your skin temperature, heart rate, breathing rate, and muscle tension. A trained biofeedback counselor then guides the patient through relaxation techniques while the patient watches the machine monitors. When heart rate or breathing rate decreases, for example, you can see it on the monitor. You learn how your body feels when your heart and breathing rate decrease. Eventually, after a number of sessions, you learn to lower your heart rate, breath rate, muscle tension, temperature, and so forth, on your own.

**breathing exercises**
These exercises involve any of various techniques for infusing the body with oxygen and energy, for the purposes of improved health and relaxation.

**breathing meditation**
This meditation involves any of various techniques of measured, controlled breathing to relax the body and improve health.

**conscious moderation**
Conscious moderation involves making a conscious effort to consume food, drink, and other resources, including money, moderately for greater inner and outer balance.

**creativity therapy**
In this therapy, you use creative expression, such as painting, writing, poetry, or playing music, as a way to release stressful feelings.

**dance**
Whether you take an organized class or go out dancing with your friends every weekend, dancing is great cardiovascular exercise and also a lot of fun.

### exercise
Exercise involves moving the body to improve health, mood, strength, flexibility, and cardiopulmonary function and to release excessive energy such as that generated by the stress response.

### friend therapy
Friend therapy is simple: Let your friends help you manage your stress! Research shows that people without social networks and friends often feel lonely but often won't admit it.

### gym/health club
This is a nice way to have lots of fitness options in one place.

### herbal medicine
Herbal remedies are taken for better health and stress resistance. Practice with caution or under the guidance of an experienced and qualified herbalist.

### journaling
Writing in a journal is a way to release stressful feelings.

### lifestyle management techniques
These involve any techniques for improving and easing daily life, including techniques for simplicity, de-cluttering, organizing, time management, relationship management, family dynamics, and self-improvement.

**massage therapy**
In massage therapy, any of various massage techniques are used to relax the muscles and free blocked energy in the body.

**meditation**
Meditation is focused concentration to gain control over the wayward mind and enhance relaxation.

**nutrition**
You should eat a variety of fresh, natural foods in moderate amounts to improve health and the body's ability to handle stress.

**pilates**
This consists of specific core-strengthening exercises performed on a mat or on special machines that concentrate on the abdominal and back muscles.

**prayer**
Prayer consists of focused, concentrated communication, a statement of intention, or the opening of the channel between you and divinity, whatever divinity is for you.

**reflexology**
Reflexology is a little like acupressure, but in reflexology, all the pressure points are in the hands and feet. The theory goes that the entire body, including all the parts, organs, and glands, is represented in a "map" on the hands and feet, and that pressure applied to the

right area of the "map" will help to balance the problem in the associated area of the body.

### relaxation techniques
These include any of many techniques for relaxing the body and mind.

### sleep
Most adults need about eight hours of sleep each day, and some need even more. Getting enough sleep is an important step toward being able to manage stress.

### swimming
Swimming is especially good for people who can't take much stress on joints, who are overweight and just beginning to exercise, or who enjoy being in the water.

### team sports
For people who like to play on a team and are motivated and energized by the energy of others, team sports can be an excellent way to get exercise and a social life at the same time.

### visualization
This is the technique of imagining something you want or a change you would like to see in yourself in order to mentally set your intention and help to effect the changes.

**vitamin/mineral therapy**
This therapy involves taking vitamins and minerals to cover your nutritional bases and protect against deficiencies for better health and a more stress-resistant body.

**walking**
A versatile exercise choice for people of any fitness level, walking is excellent for boosting mood and reducing stressful feelings as well as improving physical fitness.

**water**
To keep the body well hydrated and properly functioning, drink sixty-four to eighty ounces of water each day.

**worry control**
Worry control involves learning to recognize obsessive worrying and re-direct that energy in more positive ways.

**yoga**
Yoga is an ancient Indian method of exercise designed to "yoke" body and mind through specific postures, breathing exercises, and meditation.

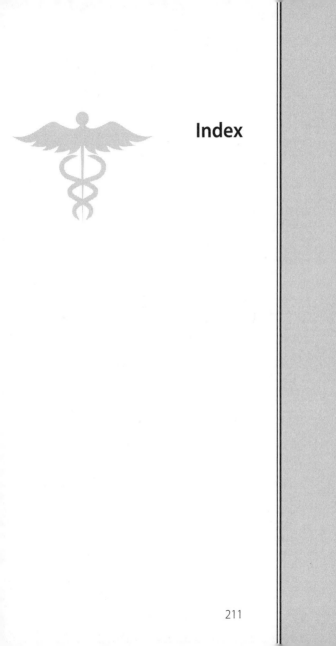

# Index